The Empath and Shadow Work

ELAINE LA JOIE

Copyright © 2013 Elaine La Joie

All rights reserved.

ISBN-10: 1491029099
ISBN-13: 978-1491029091

DEDICATION

To Greta, who I am of course NOT putting on a pedestal. You are obviously the wisest woman of your generation. Thank you for being a great mentor to one crazy Empath

CONTENTS

	Acknowledgments	i
1	Introduction	1
2	Projection and Positive and Negative Shadow	3
3	Identity and the Shadow	10
4	The Mother Wound	30
5	The Black and White Thinker	37
6	Conclusion	67

ACKNOWLEDGMENTS

I acknowledge my clients who contributed their stories to this book. It was by mentoring them through their Shadow Work that this book was born. Thank you.

1 INTRODUCTION

This book is the fourth volume of **Empath as Archetype**, a series that I began writing seven years ago to help my mostly Empath clients understand the basic concepts of shamanic work and mythic archetypes. My books are written for Empaths, but the concepts presented apply to all my clients, whether they are Empaths, friends of Empaths, or partners of Empaths. I assume that the reader has already studied the first three volumes: *the Archetypal Drama Triangle, Shamanic Energy Work, and Motivations of the Empath*. In this fourth volume I introduce Shadow Work. Shadow Work in shamanic terms means that we begin exploring the disowned parts of ourselves so that we can reclaim our personal power hidden there. Shadow Work can be painful as we grow conscious of how we have been causing trouble and pain to people around us without knowing it; we've been creating unconsciously outcomes that we do not want. The following volumes in this series will contain in depth examples of Shadow Work and the accompanying necessary shamanic healing work. Most examples are a compilation of experiences of my mostly Empath clients. In this book we will begin by looking at the typical Empath's Shadow stemming from a mother wound, in the middle of the book we will look at an extreme example of Shadow, and at the end of the book we will look at what it is like for an Empath to be the target of a non-Empath's mother wound projection.

Before we delve into Shadow Work, we must understand a very important concept in shamanism: much of our reality is created through our beliefs, whether we consciously know it or not. Our reality is strongly influenced by our perception. If our perception is clouded by distorted projections, our reality also becomes distorted. So, if we can take full responsibility for our lives, (which means stepping out of the Victim position for good) we can create lives that we really want once we clean up our distorted projections, whether they come from the family system or from our personal experience. At the same time, the Collective Consciousness or the Archetypes inform all human beings. Understanding the belief system that comes with these Archetypal forces means we can be more at choice in our own individual conscious spiritual journey.

The Victim Archetype is part of every human's experience because we come into the world as helpless infants, relying on someone imperfect to take care of us. All of us come away from our childhood experience wounded in some way. How we interpret these experiences and the conclusions we draw become our core beliefs. These beliefs become the filters through which we interpret the next experience, helping to set up our Enneagram Archetype.

The Classic Empath tends to have in common a set of original wounds and corresponding set of beliefs. Draining these wounds of emotional and energetic charge is essential so that these wounds are not projected onto the people we may meet as we go about our daily lives. We do our Shadow Work when we understand how we project our wounds and how we interpret the behavior of others in the present based on beliefs stemming from those unhealed wounds from our past. While this may sound like psychology for those readers with that background, I have observed this from my shamanic perspective, so it may not correspond exactly. Let's begin by looking at typical Empath projections.

2 PROJECTION

Projection and Positive and Negative Shadow

We all have aspects of ourselves of which we are fully conscious. At the same time, we also have those parts that are unknown to us, which is the Positive and Negative Shadow. The Negative Shadow is those parts of us that we don't like that we are not ready to see. Because we aren't ready to see these parts we tend to dislike that behavior in others with an emotional intensity out of proportion to the situation. A great way to get to know our negative shadow is to focus on someone we hate and pick out all the reasons we hate them. Chances are we are looking at parts of ourselves that we are willing to see only in the object of hatred.

The most apt examples of Negative Shadow come from those people who publicly persecute others for traits or behavior they don't like, and then it comes to light later that that the persecutor also had the trait or was caught acting out the same behavior. Many gay men not comfortable with their sexuality have bullied and even physically attacked openly gay men. Many people engaging in affairs have criticized others for their promiscuous lifestyle. Our Negative Shadows tend to make us into hypocrites.

The Positive Shadow contains those gifts within ourselves that we do not see as our own. We may admire someone for their talents in an area, not realizing that the depth of our admiration stems from the fact that we are also meant to do what they are doing. In fact, much of falling in love is seeing the positive parts of ourselves in another person. Infatuation is a common trap for Empaths. When Infatuation is understood as the projection of Positive Shadow onto the love object instead of Love, the Empath can use these powerful emotions as a Mythic Map of the inner self or the old relationship rather than as a reason to chase after the love object. Another example of Positive Shadow is admiring another for the work that he does, not realizing that we are also meant to do that work, too. Our positive shadows tend to keep us from fully experiencing our own authority and power to create.

From the shaman's perspective all of reality is contained within each of us because of our innate wholeness. Human beings tend to polarize reality and create Shadows. From the shaman's perspective our reality is based on our perception. Therefore, it is a good idea to understand our projections, or how we distort our perception. Once we do this we can begin to see ourselves and others clearly. The following are some common Empath projections.

Projection and Jealousy

I have a good friend whom I had met early on in my practice, just as I was getting started. As my practice grew, and my life grew with it, more joy, more friends, more fun, more money, and a wonderfully expansive life came through for me and for my husband. I had made a vast effort with considerable emotional and financial risk going after a dream that was non-traditional: establishing a shamanic and intuitive practice from home. My friend had seen most of the development of this lifestyle, and had expressed pride and admiration for my work. After she quit a job that was killing her soul, she began to feel more and more jealousy toward me. She was afraid that she was going to ruin the friendship between us, but felt embarrassed admitting her negative feelings to me.

When I pointed out that perhaps the jealousy stemmed from the fact that I was doing something that was very similar to what she would like to do and to have in her life, but she was as yet afraid to take significant steps, she had to admit that I was right. The jealousy melted away with the realization of a projection of Positive Shadow onto me. Jealousy had overtaken admiration because my friend was right on the cusp but afraid to step into her own path. Failure would mean not being able to claim her power that she had projected onto me. What she didn't realize was that the reaction of jealousy at the power she saw in me pointed to similar power inside of her. She could claim it at any time if she could get over the fear of it not belonging to her. I'm happy to say that my friend successfully embraced that part of her Positive Shadow, and began stepping into a healer's calling of her own, with an abundant, happy personal life attached. As a side benefit for both of us, our friendship strengthened as a result of her claiming her power hidden in that Positive Shadow. She could have used that power to destroy our friendship by acting out of her jealousy, but she did the hard work of becoming conscious of her Shadow instead.

Projecting the Past onto the Present

We project when we interpret someone's behavior based on our unhealed experiences with another person from our past, usually a parent figure. It is important for Empaths to understand the power of projection in ourselves and others, because another person's projection can literally push Empaths into behaviors that we wouldn't usually choose to do. An example would be a husband projecting his mother issues onto his Empath wife, and his wife responding as his mother would instead of how she would. This phenomenon happens to all people, not just Empaths, but because Empaths so easily match whatever vibration is needed at the time, we tend to be more susceptible than others.

Having someone in the present trigger old feelings from our past is extremely common. In fact, most interactions with others involves this projection to some degree. Any time we have a problem with another while thinking something like, "She reminds me of my mother!" most likely means we are not seeing that person clearly, but we are seeing our mother instead. Noticing within ourselves all the places that we are liable to project is extremely helpful in keeping relationships clear.

As an example, in my work I have taught small classes, and some of my personal friends have attended as students. Within the class environment, it is perfectly appropriate for me to be in the position of leader. However, outside the classroom, within a casual environment I triggered a friend's wounding with authority figures. This friend had old resentment toward her authoritarian father.

When I was in the position of teacher outside the classroom, she immediately had a problem with my behavior. Since she was projecting attributes of her father onto me she did not judge my actions fairly. Instead of my having simply answered a question for which I knew considerably more than the other people at the table, I had also committed the crime of keeping myself above my friends by not showing vulnerability.

My friend's assessment of the situation to me sounded nothing like what had actually occurred, but it did sound a lot like many of the interactions she had described with her father. Knowing what her history was, I suggested to her that perhaps she was projecting. This friend knew about the Shadow, and although it made her uncomfortable, she was willing to look more closely and see if she was projecting. Much of her anger at me dissipated when she realized it was misdirected. In this case it was very clear my friend was projecting her anger at her father onto me. However, sometimes both projection and inappropriate behavior are present, and in those cases it can be harder to sort out how much of the reaction is projection and how much of it is from the present situation. The clue that projection is in play is in the intensity of the emotional reaction.

Projection—Original Wounds Can Play Off Each Other

I had the misfortune of watching a wonderful friendship between two of my friends become completely destroyed by projection. Both women had mother issues, but both women knew about Shadow Work, and so it would seem there would be a good chance that the relationship would survive any projections. However, sometimes the original wounding can be so intense that one or both people become stuck in the projection and cannot see the situation clearly. That person can be in so much pain that the rejection of the relationship is the only way out. Empaths will commonly withdraw from others in order to escape a painful relationship, feeling completely justified in doing so, when many times an older wound, and the projection of that wound, is at work.

In this case one woman, Beth, had had a terrible time with a controlling mother figure. Beth's mother was highly critical, unsupportive, and demanded to be the center of attention. When she couldn't be the center of attention, she'd fall ill and need a trip to the emergency room with the expectation that Beth would come to the Rescue and care take her. The other woman, Liz, had mother issues, but they were the opposite. Liz's mother was checked out most of the time and so had become very passive and withdrawn. Liz had grown up feeling like she had to not only do more work in relationships, but initiate the work as well. Liz had been trained to confront problems head on as a direct result of dealing with her passive mother.

At one point Beth came home from a business trip during which she felt like she had been bossed around and made to feel second class although she had expected to be treated as an equal. Beth called Liz expecting sympathy and support. Beth theorized that she must be doing something to attract such attacks since her life seemed to be full of them. Beth, even though she was in pain, understood that here was another opportunity for Shadow Work on a core issue. Liz, trying to be sympathetic and supportive, agreed. Liz, direct as she was, suggested Beth ought to start working on her Shadow. For Beth, this triggered her original wound of being cut down by her overly critical mother when she was already down. Even though Liz did not mean it that way, Beth interpreted that comment as if Liz had meant to be critical and lay blame on Beth, even though Beth knew that very projection had been triggered.

Beth's habitual response to her mother's attacks was to withdraw to protect herself. She did so without telling Liz of her hurt feelings. To Liz, this triggered her own wounding of her mother withdrawing instead of being direct and dealing with problems as they occurred. The more Liz tried to be direct to resolve the situation with Beth, the more Beth withdrew, creating a painful spiral.

At one point, Beth consulted with me because she felt like Liz was psychically attacking her. Liz was certainly feeling angry and rejected unfairly. When I checked her, I saw Beth's lifelong Victim-ready-to-be-Bullied pattern had been triggered at work. While this wound was triggered, Beth could not but help interpret all information through the lens of her mother wound. Beth even stated, "Liz reminds me so much of my mother!" When I pointed out that that meant she most likely wasn't seeing Liz clearly, Beth agreed. But, she could not remain conscious long enough to stop her reaction and change her behavior toward Liz.

Liz on the other hand, realized that her own wounds were triggered, and managed to stop her pursuit of a resolution with Beth. She was hopeful that Beth would have space to regain a more objective view. However, the damage had been done. Beth, in the spectacularly final way that unhealed Empaths can end relationships, rejected Liz completely. In the end, the relationship failed. Not only that, but friends Liz and Beth had in common also became guilty by association, and Beth let those relationships go, too. Beth had managed to isolate herself from the very support that she craved.

How could this situation have turned out differently, especially given that Beth was aware that she was projecting onto Liz? This is where understanding the Drama Triangle is so important. If Beth could have seen that she was firmly in the Victim position and had put Liz into the Bully position, she might have been able to step away and see that she didn't necessarily want the Drama to play itself out as it will do when we are not conscious of a Victim stance. Eventually the Victim turns to Bully, and feels justified in doing so. If she could have told herself that her mother issue was in play, and that any perception she had was going to be colored by that, she might have been able to step back from her projection and instead question whether Liz was really attacking her, even though it felt that way.

But unfortunately, once Beth justified her Victim position, she cast everyone around her into Bully roles and hunkered down. The real key to healing here is looking directly at the Mother Wound, which is fueling the projection and the accompanying emotions. Healing the root cause, sometimes with help of Soul Retrieval work, and draining the emotional charge prevents the projection from occurring again with destructive intensity. For most people such healing takes time and practice. Beth had taken the first step of being conscious: she knew she was projecting. The next step is choosing to step out of Victim and take responsibility for casting others into the other roles. She wasn't able to do that in this situation, but Life will give her another chance to try again.

Life does bring us repeated chances to change our perceptions and heal those wounds that lead to the projections for the very reason that our projections create much of our lives. In other words, we unconsciously set up opportunities to experience the pattern again and again. If our projections lead to a happy life, that is great, but when our projections lead to a pattern of hurtful behavior or repeated unhappy outcomes, we know a root trauma and faulty belief system is at work.

Our next example, although extreme, illustrates how our Shadows can create the exact opposite of what we intend. Remember, the Shadow begins by dividing reality into good and bad. It grows when we begin denying our feelings to the point that we must project those feelings outward. Let's take a look at the Shadow of a woman who had so completely divided the world into Black and White that she isolated herself and her family from the love and community she had been taught to value.

3 IDENTITY AND THE SHADOW

One requirement of doing Shadow Work is the willingness to feel momentarily bad about ourselves without defense. We can then get to know our Shadows by looking at behavior that we deplore, especially actions that we think we would never take while experiencing the accompanying shame. We cannot do Shadow Work unless we are willing to feel shame, fear, anger, embarrassment, humiliation, and pain. It is important to realize that every person is capable of horrendous acts, thoughts, and petty feelings given the right circumstances. The more we deny our inner psychopath, the more likely it is that we will be susceptible to acting out that which we claim we would never do. We will either justify our actions, or worse, deny them entirely.

We have all met people who we know will never change because they are so stuck in their patterns. These people think that everyone but themselves are wrong, that they are the only blameless, reasonable people in the world. These people can have difficulty admitting that they can make mistakes because of a belief system that makes them identify with being good or perfect. Evidence that they are not good or perfect creates feelings of shame or fear, which they are not strong enough internally to bear.

Dealing with such people can be extremely frustrating and baffling to Empaths. I had a client who found herself in this situation with one of her neighbors. Claire's small neighborhood, which was full of families with small children of the same age, looked idyllic. The children all played together and for the most part got along well, except for one family. This family consisted of three boys seven years and younger, a home-maker, and a father who was often away on business. The mother, Bambi, let her children run around the neighborhood from an extremely young age without supervision. Claire told me that one of her first interactions with Bambi foreshadowed the problems she would later have with this family. The first time Claire met Bambi Claire and her husband were outside watching their little boy, who was only a toddler. Their neighbor's oldest son, Jack, who was around three years old at the time, was at the end of their driveway. This gregarious little boy had a great time describing his bike to my client and her husband. Bambi came out to ask Jack to come inside to watch the baby while she took a shower. Claire was taken aback when Jack ignored his mother even after several attempts to catch his attention. Claire was further horrified when Bambi gave up and walked back inside instead of picking up her son and taking him with her. At that point it was clear that Bambi had unknowingly trained her son by the early age of three to ignore her. Bambi was either too tired or unwilling to make the effort to follow through on her instructions.

At first most of the other parents in the neighborhood had sympathy for Bambi After all, they knew how difficult raising small children was even with two involved parents, while this family had just one involved parent. They were willing to give her the benefit of the doubt. Bambi's parenting skills never improved as the children grew up, and the other parents grew frustrated and then resentful. Bambi did not seem to understand that by letting her kids run around the neighborhood without supervision that she was putting a burden on her neighbors. It might have been different if her children were well behaved, but since the boys did not listen to the adults, and the middle son, Jason, was sullen and angry to the point of talking back to the parents and bullying the other children, the parents began dreading the appearance of these boys.

Attachment to a Role as an Identity can Create Shadow

My Empath client had two children who were high energy like the neighbor's boys. However, Claire knew that because she was an Empath that she could not handle the demands of supervising her children for hours at a time every day without help. It was simply too much stimulation and tedium combined with the requirement to stay alert and present. As an Empath Claire needed her downtime and her quiet time or she would not have the patience to treat her children well when she was the sole caretaker. She and her husband had hired a nanny to help her out during the day as she pursued a career as an artist, even though this was a financial burden for them. They realized that having a competent nanny who thrived on rambunctious boy-energy was the best option for raising their children who were still under school age.

The important difference between Claire and Bambi was that Claire was not invested in her role of mother as an identity. Therefore, she could see what her natural limits were as a parent. Claire consciously knew she needed help and did not judge herself. She understood that she had a responsibility to her children (and to everyone who came into contact with them) to make sure that they were raised with loving but firm limits. Claire's children would internalize those limits into healthy respect for their fellow human beings as they matured. She also knew that setting limits and enforcing them was not easy, but that it had to be done despite any discomfort to herself. Claire understood her responsibilities as a parent.

Bambi on the other hand had an image of what motherhood and raising a family should look like. She was invested in this image as her identity. Bambi both imagined and also believed that for her raising children should be easy and that she should love and want to be with them all the time. Being a mother was more than her job; it was her raison d'etre. If she wasn't a good mother, then she didn't have anything else in her life. Bambi was also part of a church that emphasized the importance of close-knit family and community. Her personal beliefs coupled with her group's beliefs led her to push all her negative feelings about motherhood into the Shadow as wrong and therefore unwanted. The truth is that all of us sometimes feel frustrated, angry, and out of control when it comes to raising our children. But Bambi's image required her to handle any family crisis with equanimity, patience, and no complaints. Her belief system did not allow her to have mixed feelings about motherhood. Most people are conscious of their mixed feelings, which means that they can do a good job monitoring their behavior most of the time, and so the average human being turns out functional.

Early on in their relationship Bambi told Claire that she wanted to have five boys so that they would come home for Christmas with their wives to visit her. Claire thought this was completely crazy, given that it was so difficult to raise the three Bambi already had. How would two more fit into the mix? These idyllic visions of the far future meant that Bambi distracted herself from the ongoing difficulties in the present. On top of this, Bambi's middle child, Jason, was angry and sullen. Jason had taken to pulling the legs off of grasshoppers and spiders, but Bambi's attitude was that boys would be boys. When Jack, her oldest boy, beat up on Jason, her response was that boys would be boys. Then Bambi would take her youngest boy inside and leave the older two boys to their own devices. The boys roamed the neighborhood doing whatever they liked, and ignored anyone who objected to their behavior. They had so much practice ignoring their mother that she had trained them to ignore everyone else too. When Jason came outside to play, he saw several children his age also out to play, but always with either one parent, both parents or a nanny. On some level, Jason was picking up the hidden messages, "These other kids are important because their parents spend time with them, but I am not important enough for my mother to spend time with me," and "Everyone is afraid of me or unhappy to see me."

What Does Not Fit the Image is Pushed into the Shadow

Bambi had told Claire that Jason had spent three months in the hospital beginning when he was a few months old because he had caught his older brother's cold and she had not known to be careful with her newborn. Jason had of course experienced extreme Soul Loss as an infant by being placed in the NICU. His life had been saved, but his Soul had been wounded. Bambi had unintentionally let him down, and had been required to leave him alone. It was understandable that Jason had subconscious beliefs around abandonment, needing to be mothered, and feeling extremely angry about the isolation he had suffered. In the present Bambi's neglecting to supervise her children combined with the other parents' frustration and exasperation at his behavior only served to reinforce this young child's belief system.

Claire had spoken to Bambi about unconventional solutions to her son's behavioral issues, which Bambi fearfully described as oppositional defiance disorder. Bambi seemed open to alternative methods of healing, including seeing a classical homeopath or a shaman for Soul Retrieval work. However, she never followed through on taking any action. Part of taking responsibility meant feeling the despair and frustration that Bambi was repressing. When we are healthy we use such emotions as fuel to change our situation. But Bambi was invested in living an idyllic domestic life, which meant not feeling despair and frustration for long, even if it meant not seeking help for her son. Even though she consciously knew that Jason was angry, and that Jack was disrespectful to adults and had only learned to behave once he started school, Bambi avoided staying conscious and prayed that somehow things would work themselves out. Bambi did the classic move of burying her head in the sand, ignoring the effect that this would have not just on her sons, but on her neighbors as well.

However, when we push our negative emotions into the Shadow, that means that we will begin to justify behaviors that protect our self-image as good for everyone around us. Bambi pushed her knowledge that her boys were hard for her to deal with into the Shadow. To prevent herself from dealing with her feelings (and her difficult boys), she sent them out unsupervised to play. If she didn't see their behavior, then she didn't have to deal with their behavior or her feelings. If anyone complained about her children, she could interpret her boys' behavior in a way that suited her since she did not see it with her own eyes. To justify not supervising her kids, Bambi told herself and her neighbors that she believed in her children learning by experience. Bambi had convinced herself that her bad parenting, which protected her from her own uncomfortable feelings, was the best parenting she could do for her children! If Bambi hadn't been invested in being a perfect mother, she might have been able to tell herself that sending her kids out to play unsupervised was not the optimal solution, but it was the best she could do at the time given her resources. She might have been more willing to have her neighbors help and input as well.

Projecting Unwanted Negative Feelings Outwards

When we push our negative emotions into the Shadow, we begin projecting those feelings onto the people around us. Bambi was frustrated by how difficult parenting was for her. She was secretly fearful that she wasn't living up to her image as a good mother, but denied this fear. Instead of dealing with her own frustration toward her kids, she interpreted her neighbors' exasperation as hostility toward her kids, when in fact the neighbors were frustrated with Bambi and her parenting and understood that the boys were innocent. When Bambi's neighbors began to give her feedback that her children were out of control, she became defensive. Her neighbors were only confirming what Bambi herself had seen, but she had pushed what she had seen out of her consciousness. Now when Bambi became defensive she thought it was in defense of her children when in actuality she was defensive of her self-image as a good mother. Her anger at her neighbors subconsciously stemmed from that threat rather than the neighbors' view of her children. Consciously Bambi focused on how hard her neighbors were on her kids, while her neighbors simply wanted her to do something about her kids. Unfortunately, for Bambi to do actual good parenting, she would have to come into contact with all her repressed feelings about motherhood that did not fit her self-image. Her own Shadow made her project her negativity on top of her neighbors' responses, making their feedback seem more negative.

What the neighbors saw was a woman that was peculiarly dismissive or defensive. When Bambi was in a good mood, she would excuse her boys' unruly and sometimes violent behavior as "boys will be boys" and would ignore her neighbors' complaints as if they were of no consequence. However, when she was feeling at her limit emotionally, after being confronted by one neighbor over the same behavior she would not speak to all the neighbors for days, giving them angry looks. When under stress Bambi showed her underlying fear of being judged by her whole neighborhood as a neglectful parent. Bambi could not shrug off their opinion of her as she came in close contact with her own negative emotions about parenthood. Bambi started giving her neighbors the cold shoulder for no apparent reason. The neighbors began checking in on each other to see which one had confronted Bambi this time. Finally my client, Claire, and her neighbors accepted that Bambi was unpredictable and ineffectual and began holding the unruly boys to their own rules. For a while this worked well, given that the neighbors had similar expectations of behavior from their children and were consistent with all the children. None of the other parents had any problems with another neighbor disciplining their kids. Bambi's younger boys started to respond well to limits, to being noticed and to being held accountable by the other adults. Jason, who was the likeliest to act out his anger, even began cuddling in Claire's lap.

However, it didn't take long for Bambi to object to the neighbors telling her kids what to do. Her eldest boy, Jack, complained that the other adults were mean to him and his brothers. This report made Bambi angry and frustrated with her neighbors over her children's perceived mistreatment. She refused to see that by not supervising her kids, she was leaving her neighbors in a bind in which they had to deal with her children instead of her, but she wouldn't let them deal with her kids. She heard the neighbors scold her kids with frustration in their voices. Some of that frustration she projected onto her neighbors. In other words, instead of Bambi hearing the normal frustration that comes with parenting, Bambi had so repressed hers into the Shadow that her own frustration had nowhere to go but into distorting her neighbors' reactions. As a consequence Bambi heard more frustration than her neighbors were feeling. Hearing that frustration infuriated her because she believed that good parents should not get angry at children. She had pushed her anger into the Shadow as wrong, and so it was easy for her to see her neighbors as wrong for being angry instead of curbing her boys' behavior. She blamed her neighbors for being impatient and disrespectful towards her children, when in reality she had done nothing to ensure that her kids were respectful toward the other children and adults. Bambi could not see or take responsibility for how she had created the uncomfortable situation for everyone. More importantly Bambi could not fix the situation because making it better would mean that she would have to come in contact with her fears about how she wasn't living up to her ideal of motherhood.

Reality Checks are Unwelcome

The situation escalated one evening when Claire was out with her two boys and her husband in their driveway, preparing to leave for an event. Her husband had their younger boy in his lap as he helped his toddler put on his shoes. Jason, who was at the top of the driveway with his scooter, watched her husband and son's interaction jealously. Jason jumped on his scooter and deliberately tried to run down her toddler. Instead Jason hit her husband's shins. Her husband, reacting and in pain, swatted Jason away, scolding, "No crashing, Jason, that hurt!" Jason, probably having never experienced corporal punishment before, threw down his scooter and ran to tell his parents. Claire turned to her neighbors, who were also out in her driveway, and asked what they should do. Her neighbors shrugged, thinking that it was a reasonable way for her husband to react. Maybe now Jason would think twice before acting out his anger.

When Claire's husband went to talk to Jason's father about the incident, he was careful not to blame Jason and to take all responsibility for the outcome on himself. Jason's father, Dick, seemed to respond well and to put the matter behind him. Claire's husband had already decided that from now on he would take his boys inside or to the park if he saw Bambi's boys outside. He wanted to avoid a future incident. However, Bambi confronted Claire the next morning, wanting to make sure that there wasn't tension between the neighbors so that she could continue to live out her fantasy that she was a good neighbor and good parent. Claire, like most Empaths, told Bambi in authentic fashion that of course there was tension between the neighbors. Bambi was allowing her children to run around the neighborhood unsupervised, Claire's nanny was fed up with having to watch four boys instead of the two she was paid for, and now Jason had deliberately tried to run down her toddler with his scooter. Luckily her husband had been in the way. Bambi immediately went from a friendly, conciliatory attitude to a very angry one. She responded that Claire could not know that that had been Jason's intention. Claire pointed out that Bambi certainly could not know because Bambi hadn't been in the driveway.

Bambi retorted that Claire should have just come to get her when the incident had happened instead of hitting Jason. Claire, exasperated, explained again that this had been a gut reaction in the moment, in order to protect her child, and that Jason had barely been hit. Neither she nor her husband was going to allow Jason to hurt another child in their presence if they could help it. If Bambi didn't like that, then she should keep Jason at home. Bambi then told Claire that she and Dick believed that their children should learn by experience, and not be "helicoptered" like the other parents were doing to their children. Claire replied that Bambi should have no complaints then: Jason got the lesson that if he hurt someone with his scooter, the hurt person might retaliate. It was a natural and logical consequence. Jason was now unlikely to try and run down her toddler while adults were outside. Bambi she had to come over and do something when she heard that someone was laying hands on her child. Claire was momentarily stunned by this hypocrisy, but then told Bambi that if Bambi had so little trust in her and her husband as good people, then she really should keep Jason at home and away from such dangerous neighbors. Claire also said that she could ask the other neighbors what had happened. They would tell her the same story and that it was not that big a deal.

Bambi recoiled at this statement. Instead of reassuring Bambi, Claire unintentionally threatened Bambi's fantasy of neighborly friendliness and community. Bambi's repressed fear had been confirmed. All the parents who had seen the incident agreed that Jason was a bad kid and that Bambi was a negligent parent. Claire, being an Empath, felt Bambi's suddenly unsuppressed despair. Even though Claire was exasperated and furious with Bambi, she had the momentary urge to hug her. Claire reminded Bambi that she needed to get Jason help for his behavioral issues. He was now trying to hurt other children. The situation was serious! Claire told Bambi that everyone understood that her raising three boys mostly on her own was difficult and so of course they understood her need for a break. However, not supervising them at all was taking a toll on everyone. Bambi angrily retorted that she couldn't afford a nanny like Claire, and that Claire didn't understand what it meant to be a real mother. Claire noted the jealousy and the judgment. Bambi must have noted it as well because she immediately left.

What Claire didn't understand was that Bambi had come over expecting an apology and expecting to be treated as the wronged parent. Bambi expected Claire to behave as Claire's husband had with Dick. Claire, being an Empath, was not about to hide her true thoughts and feelings and play into Bambi's fantasy. Claire, being an Empath, assumed Bambi would do what she could to fix the problem once reality was pushed clearly and forcefully in her face and down her throat. Claire did not understand that Bambi's whole purpose was to avoid reality at all costs, even to the cost of her sons and to her relationship with her neighbors. Claire had told Bambi that all the rest of the neighbors shared her opinion in order to make the point that Bambi should take Jason's behavior seriously. However, given Bambi's over-sensitivity about her poor mothering, this statement felt like an attack to Bambi.

Basically Bambi had been subconsciously resentful that her neighbors were destroying her happy image of herself as a good mother and her family as a good family. She unconsciously had blamed the other parents for their opinion of her rather than face reality. Now Claire had spoken aloud what Bambi most feared. Now in order to deny reality effectively Bambi had to see her neighbors as bad people. If her neighbors were bad people, then she didn't have to take their opinions seriously. Bambi had to resort to black and white thinking in order to keep her version of reality intact, which is a sure way of creating an even bigger Shadow. It was easy for her to think of Claire and her husband as bad people given that Claire's husband had swatted Jason. The other neighbors thought Bambi's conclusion was ironic because Claire's husband was known as the most gentle and friendly dad to all the kids on the block, and Claire was known as the mom most likely to give the kids treats and presents.

The Neighbors are Cast as Villains

A few years later Bambi's children were still out of control and growing older. Luckily for Claire and the neighbors, Jack and Jason had been told to leave a wide berth around Claire's family. Since Claire and her family were usually out daily with their neighbors, they didn't see as much of Bambi's boys. The few times they did see the kids, the boys would run away or not make eye contact. If Bambi was out with her boys, she deliberately turned her back on Claire. Bambi was required to walk Jason, who was in Kindergarten, to the bus stop. Claire, out there with her boys, was given the cold shoulder. Claire shrugged, disappointed and exasperated. Bambi also gave the other neighbors the cold shoulder; they had all been lumped together as bad people.

Once the boys were in school and other families besides the neighbors started complaining of her boys' behavior, Bambi ignored their complaints as well and found ways to excuse her boys. When Jason bashed another boy in the head on the school bus, and that boy was no longer allowed to play with her son, Bambi told herself that the hurt child had misrepresented the incident to his mother. Bambi once again downplayed her child's angry and violent behavior so that she wouldn't have to deal with reality and her own repressed feelings. Bambi simply could not deal with her Shadow, or the fact that she did not have the domestic life she believed she must live up to. Eventually none of the families with children the same age in Bambi's neighborhood would allow their kids to play with her kids.

The Situation Escalates

This neighborhood backed up to a green space that some of the older children used for shooting practice. These teens had been trained by their parents, wore all the protective gear, and acted responsibly. With no one their age to play with, Bambi's boys began spending time with the older kids. Bambi allowed her boys, the oldest under ten years, to have air rifles. The neighbors were unhappy with this development, but the boys stayed in the green space with the teenagers when the rifles came out. One evening Claire was sitting in her driveway with three other families while their kids played together. Jack came out with his air rifle and stood with the kids in the driveway. When one of the parents asked Jack whether the rifle was loaded, the boy turned toward his younger brother, who was standing between two of the other children, and shot Jason in the face. Jason ran inside to tell his mother as Jack ran after him. The parents sat in the driveway, stunned. Any of their kids could have been hurt.

A few minutes later Jack came out to play again. One of the fathers approached him and told Jack that if he saw him with the gun again that he was going to take it away from him and break it in two. This parent was understandably angry and frustrated given that his child could have been shot, could have lost an eye, or could have been otherwise injured. Jack ran back inside the house. The parents then discussed what they could do to protect their children given how out of hand the boys had become, and given that despite all their being outside, the children had only with luck escaped being hurt. Bambi, as usual, was nowhere to be seen. They decided that even if they confronted Bambi, given their years of dealing with her, that she still would not do anything about her boys' behavior. They did not know what to do next and sat in the driveway together feeling defeated.

Imagine their surprise when Bambi came outside with her three boys and proceeded to yell at them for threatening Jack. The father who had scolded Jack had not mentioned to the others that he had reprimanded the boy, so the rest of the parents looked at Bambi in amazement. They had been expecting an apology, and yet here she was yelling at them. When one of the mothers responded that they did not know what Bambi was talking about, Bambi immediately assumed that her neighbor was lying to protect her husband. She gathered her children to go inside and away from her dishonest and threatening neighbors. Bambi did not ask her neighbors what had happened, and she made no apology for Jack shooting off his gun with the other kids just a few feet away. Bambi had no grasp of how she and her boys were affecting the neighborhood's peace and safety, and honestly did not care. Bambi was so bent on protecting her boys from the "threatening" father, that she behaved in a completely baffling and crazy manner, which served to reinforce her own conclusion that she was the only honest, loving parent in the neighborhood.

Instead of Bambi being out in my client's driveway enjoying the summer evening with the rest of the families, she had created a situation in which she had isolated herself. Bambi had to hunker down inside her house, while sending her boys out to play so she wouldn't have to deal with them or her neighbors. Instead of being part of a community that valued children, which she had been taught to value within her own family and church, she had created a situation in which her own children had become a menace. Because Bambi would not deal with her feelings and because she had pushed so many of her feelings, thoughts, and behaviors into the Shadow, she was creating the opposite of what she wanted in life. In fact, Bambi's neighbors had created a wonderful community in which they shared celebrating birthdays and holidays while enjoying each other's different personalities. They had created community within a stable and loving framework of respect, friendliness and good boundaries. Bambi's neighbors had created the real deal, while Bambi thought she had the real deal but was in reality isolated with ill-behaved children.

After Bambi yelled at her neighbors, they decided that they needed to bring in extra help. The situation had deteriorated to the point now that instead of being irritated and inconvenienced, their children were in danger while Bambi had somehow made herself the wronged party in the air rifle incident. Technically, shooting an air rifle within city limits was illegal. So, Claire asked the police to talk to Bambi and make sure she understood the seriousness of the situation without filing a formal complaint against her. The neighbors thought that this would make a difference. However, a few days later, the mostly absent boys' father, Dick, confronted the father who had told Jack that he would take the air rifle away from him if he saw it again. Dick told him that he could have him arrested for theft if he took his child's toy away. The other parents listened to Dick make this ridiculous statement and were flabbergasted. The father replied that he wasn't planning on keeping the rifle and he would of course give it back to Dick in such a situation. He then asked Dick whether the offense of taking away the air rifle was more serious than his son shooting off the air rifle with other kids in the line of fire. Dick replied that he wasn't going to talk about that, and that he was here to talk about the father threatening Jack.

At that point Claire interrupted and asked what had been done to make sure that a similar incident would not happen again. Dick told Claire that he wasn't talking to her and that he was talking to her neighbor. Claire asked Dick if he understood that his own son had shot his other son while two of their kids were standing on either side of Jason. Dick told Claire that her husband should have gone to jail two years ago for assaulting Jason, but they hadn't called the police. Dick then told his neighbors that their calling the police was escalating the situation and that one of them would eventually go to jail if they kept it up. The neighbors listened to this assertion with disbelief. None of them had broken the law, but this man's son had, and yet he was threatening them with jail! He was threatening Claire's husband over another incident in which Claire's husband was simply trying to protect himself and his child! Dick did not stop to get the facts from the people who had witnessed the event, instead he tried to intimidate them, which was in fact escalating the situation.

Bambi then told her neighbors that she had laughed when the police officer came to talk to her because it was so ridiculous that they would waste the officer's time with such a minor incident. Bambi had no idea that this police officer had told Claire that she should go ahead and file the formal complaint rather than have him waste time just issuing a warning. He had seen enough of these incidents to know that an injury would be next. The officer actually thought Bambi was a negligent parent. Bambi then complained that she had to warn all the other parents who let their teens play with air rifles about Claire's unreasonableness, not knowing that Claire had already spoken to these families about the air rifle incident and their decision to bring in the police. These other families were also baffled by Bambi's permissiveness but felt sorry for her boys and allowed their teenagers to take them in. Bambi had no idea of how she was perceived, even by the neighbors who liked her boys. Dick then told his neighbors that he didn't like to get phone calls from his distraught wife that they were scaring and threatening his children when he was away from home. He completely missed the point that his wife and his children had scared and threatened his neighbors and their children!

When Claire responded that they were not their enemies, they were neighbors, the couple looked at her in shock. Bambi and Dick both said that they did not think of their neighbors that way. Neither could see that their actions showed their hostility and their unwillingness to treat their neighbors' concerns respectfully or seriously. They were invested in thinking of themselves as great parents and good people, and so could not risk seeing their hostility because good people did not get hostile according to their belief system. Dick thought he was completely justified in attempting to intimidate his neighbors in defense of his put-upon wife and children. Bambi thought she was completely in the right in thinking Claire's asking for help from the police was over the top. Their complaint was that their neighbors were unfair and disrespectful to their children, and if the neighbors would just leave the disciplining to them, all would be well. Both Dick and Bambi completely ignored the fact that their eldest son had shot another child without any thought or any remorse, or any consequences. Bambi and Dick could not see that they were failing their children by failing to discipline them, and as a consequence creating a dangerous situation for the entire neighborhood.

Claire then told Dick that she was counting on him to take care of the situation, given that she knew Bambi wouldn't take care of it. He looked at her confusedly and asked, "What situation?" She told him, with considerable exasperation, that she expected him to make sure his kids did not have access to the air rifles without adult supervision. Finally Dick said he would take care of it. He told Claire that she should just come and talk directly to them if there was a problem. When Claire and the other neighbors explained to him that Bambi had walked away without getting all the facts, and that that was an indication that she was not interested in talking to them, he began to look uncomfortable. Claire asked him what they should do if he was away on business and Bambi refused to talk to them or deal with her children. Bambi then protested that she had come outside and apologized to them before asking them not to threaten Jack. Claire and her neighbors could not believe Bambi's blatant distortion of events. The whole reason that the neighbors had sat there in shock was because they had been expecting an apology and instead Bambi had yelled at them for being the wrong doers. In Bambi's mind she had apologized and addressed their concerns, when in reality she hadn't in front of eight other adults. But Bambi believed her version of events completely and thought the other parents were the crazy ones.

Bambi then said that she had told her boys to avoid Claire's children, and that it had been hard on her to keep her boys confined to her own yard while the rest of the kids played together. Bambi told Claire that there were different styles of parenting and that Claire did not respect hers. Bambi complained that the neighbors were mean and disrespectful to her kids. Bambi told Claire that Claire should come tell her about any problem with her boys so that she could do the disciplining, not Claire. Claire told Bambi that Bambi had been rude and unfriendly to her for a couple of years, so she didn't want to come talk to her about her unruly children when it was obvious that Bambi was hostile. Bambi reacted in surprise and claimed that she had never been rude or hostile. She said that she was simply defensive when it came to her boys being treated unfairly. The rest of her neighbors at that moment completely gave up on Bambi as a rational human being. All of them had been snubbed or had been on the receiving end of Bambi's unpredictable silent treatment.

Bambi's version of reality was completely skewed. Bambi was angry and had behaved angrily, but because her belief system around what it meant to be a good person did not allow for anger or rudeness, she was completely unconscious of her angry behavior and how that affected her neighbors. Claire suggested that perhaps Bambi could do an even better job of keeping her children away since she thought the rest of them were mean and disrespectful. When Bambi saw that Claire was not going to budge on her opinion or her actions, and that being intimidated by her husband did not work either, she went home and hunkered down. The result was that Claire and her neighbors saw less of this family while Bambi and Dick also briefly tried to be friendly and polite in passing.

Strong Boundaries the Only Solution

The neighbors decided that if any other dangerous incidents happened that they would bring the police in immediately and let them deal with this family. Bambi had pushed so much into the Shadow that she had made her neighbors into villains and had isolated herself. Not only that but she showed that she lived in a conveniently simple world in which there were only a few good people, including her, and the rest of the population was untrustworthy. However, the most unfortunate part of this story is that she believed herself to be a great mother, when in fact she was the opposite. While her three boys had started out innocent, they were growing up with no idea of their effect on other people, and they had been trained not to care. Bambi had done nothing to prepare them to navigate the hard consequences they were sure to run into as teenagers and as young men. Bambi was the worst sort of hypocrite in saying that she wanted her children to learn by hard experience, and yet she interfered with that hard experience by defending her children from the honest reactions of others while the children were still young enough to be properly trained.

This is the nature of Shadow: Bambi literally could not see that she was neglectful, rude, and failing her boys because she was so invested in her identity as a good mother. She could not bear her feelings of shame and fear for not living up to her ideal. In order to protect herself from her feelings she made everyone on the outside the problem instead of dealing with her own internal punishing belief system and its accompanying feelings of shame and fear. Avoiding shame and fear completely motivated Bambi, but it was totally hidden from her. Maintaining her identity was her main motivation, not actually doing the work to be a good mother and to have a great family life.

How Bambi can Heal

Bambi's Shadow was extreme in this example, but it is possible for her to heal. Given Bambi's personal beliefs and the expectations of her church, Bambi was held prisoner by a punishing belief system that governed her by fear and shame. The first, always required step in true healing for Bambi, or for anyone, is admitting to herself that she has a problem and that she is the source of her problem. As we already saw, this is very unlikely. If Bambi was able to admit she had a problem, then Shamanic work is probably the fastest path to deep change for her.

Underworld Work would help Bambi dismantle the belief that she was a good person only if she adhered to a set of rules that allowed only for positive and virtuous thoughts and feelings. The benefit of this faulty belief is that it leads to Bambi having a relentlessly sunny and idyllic self-image. However, the trade-off is that the exterior world will seem overly hostile and critical towards her and her boys. Ultimately the reason to choose a belief system that allows both the black and the white is that this inner belief actually matches outer reality and will better enable a person to create their desires externally.

After the Energy Work settled, Bambi could then start taking baby steps to experience these long repressed feelings. The more Bambi could come in touch with those feelings of despair and anger, the less she would project those outwards onto her neighbors, and then the less the world in general would feel like an unfriendly place. Without the Underworld Work, healing for Bambi is bound to be emotionally painful and perhaps impossible. But it is the very step of allowing those painful and uncomfortable emotions that opens the door to true healing.

Another belief that needs reworking is the notion that Bambi's only value is as a mother, homemaker, and good community member. If Bambi can release herself from the investment in this role as an identity and see herself as a worthwhile person with many roles to play and gifts to offer, she will be better able to internally withstand seeing those places where she is not living up to her role as mother. In Bambi's case she will also need to forgive herself for helping to create boys who are likely to grow into young men who will have a negative impact on the people around them. However, her own healing could change this outcome by allowing her to have a more real and balanced relationship with her boys. Her willingness to deal with reality and see them clearly will lead to her possibly finding real help for Jason and disciplining her children with loving limits.

How to Tell if You Have a Hefty Shadow like Bambi

Spotting our Shadow by definition is difficult for the reason that it is hidden from view, and that we are invested in keeping it unconscious. How can we truly know if we are creating out of the Shadow, or if the person we are dealing with is the one creating out of his Shadow? After all, everyone has a Shadow.

In Bambi's case it is easy for her neighbors to spot her Shadow because they were all having the same problems with her. Usually it is a sure sign that our Shadow is running amok if we get the same response from different people in similar situations. Bambi might have clued in that she was the source of the problem given that four other families had the same reaction to her parenting. Later teachers at school complained about her boys, and other families not in the immediate neighborhood also complained. When the external world shows us an unwelcome outcome that repeats three times in similar yet different situations, it's usually because we are creating out of our Shadows and hidden beliefs rather than consciously.

Another clue is hypocrisy. If we find ourselves complaining of other people's behavior but excusing or justifying the same behavior in ourselves, that is a sure sign our Shadow is in play. Notice that Bambi's Shadow was so great it led her to interpret her neighbors' behavior as dangerous and untrustworthy when in fact this is what her neighbors thought of her.

An additional clue is that we create the opposite of our desires.

Bambi's Shadow was so extreme that she created the exact opposite of what she valued. Instead of creating loving family and community, she created a situation in which she was the source and cause of worry and strife for her neighbors, and so was excluded from their community.

How the Empath can Interact with Someone like Bambi

Most Empaths are like Claire in that they would automatically assume that Bambi would want to fix situations that have a negative impact on others even if it means making themselves uncomfortable. However someone like Bambi is invested in not feeling emotionally uncomfortable. While Claire can walk through her own internal emotional minefield, Bambi has to keep it simple. Bambi is not strong enough to handle dark emotions like Claire.

Bambi is overly sensitive to the reactions of others with regard to her boys' behavior and her parenting. What this means is that even if someone approaches Bambi about her kids' behavior and is completely neutral, Bambi, because she projects her negativity outward, does not see the other person as neutral, but rather she sees the other person's response to her as negative.

Claire and her neighbors could have been actively friendly and encouraging with Bambi. However, for most Empaths such behavior feels false, and they simply cannot do it. Being polite while actually disliking someone is hard enough for Empaths as it is. But for the non-Empath a good approach in dealing with someone like Bambi is to be more positive than neutral or polite while maintaining firm boundaries. For Empaths, it might be helpful to approach dealing with someone like Bambi as a practice in non-engagement. Empaths tend to want to interact authentically and engage emotionally. When dealing with someone with such a large Shadow, this is incredibly dangerous. Empaths should therefore be careful to only share the limited sunny emotions that someone like Bambi can handle while maintaining extremely strong boundaries, which might also feel unnatural to the Empath.

If the relationship has deteriorated to the point that Claire and her neighbors experienced, then a plan of protection is important. The neighbors had already decided to bring in the authorities if any other incidents occurred. They did not let their children play outside unless one of the parents was present. I also instructed Claire on how to put up protection altars for her family and for the neighbors who were open to it, and I installed energetic protections on their home.

Conclusion

When we actively deny our feelings we begin denying reality. We create a bigger and bigger Shadow. The more reality that we push into the Shadow, the less able we are to deal with our lives effectively. The more we avoid dealing with our Shadow, the more crazy-making we appear to others. Without knowing it we will tend to make life difficult for the people around us, like Bambi. When we are invested in an image of ourselves as our identity, we push what doesn't fit our self-image into the Shadow. If we need to keep this image intact, we will be unable to examine ourselves and our behavior. We will have a hard time seeing the effect of our actions on others around us, and other people's behavior will not make sense to us. It is important that we get to know our Shadow so that we can enjoy our lives and anticipate our effect on other people. We all have wondered how crazy-making people can do what they do with no shame or self-regulation. In Bambi's case this was due to her hefty Shadow.

The saddest part of this example is that it shows how a mother can unintentionally and unconsciously inflict a deep wound on a child while thinking she is a great mother. That child will then carry that wound forward into adulthood. At the end of this book we will look at how a man with a wound like Jason's tends to project that wound onto the women around him, causing him to predictably and repeatedly destroy his relationships with women, and how he can heal that wound. But first, let's explore more about how the typical Empath's mother wound tends to play out, and how the Empath can heal.

4 THE MOTHER WOUND

As stated early in the book, every human being carries the archetype of Victim given the nature of the human experience. We come into the world completely helpless, completely dependent on another flawed human being to take care of us and to meet all of our needs. For most of us, our mothers have a huge influence on how strongly this Archetype manifests within us. If our needs weren't met adequately, we tend to have big mother wounds that play out in various ways, depending on what subconscious beliefs develop, and from those, what Enneagram Archetype we take on. Many Empaths are disillusioned with both parents, but we tend to be more forgiving toward our fathers than our mothers if we are women, and visa versa if we are men. If our mothers were inadequate nurturers, as Empaths we tend to go looking for nurturing from other teachers and gurus, and we tend to want to build an emotional and special bond with that new mother figure. Usually that figure is a woman, but it can be a man, if that man has nurturing qualities. (We will talk about father wounds in a future book on romantic relationships)

In my personal experience, and in working with clients, the unfolding of a mother wound projection is the most destructive pattern in relationships. My intention is to give Empaths information and resources so that we can do as much as possible to resolve our personal mother wounds and thus prevent a painful relationship breakdown. But then, the next step is to help Empaths avoid becoming the mother-substitute for someone else and have that relationship fail as well. It is a predictable outcome that such a relationship, if the other person does not get a handle on the wound, will fall apart, usually drastically and painfully. Depending on the Enneagram Archetype of the other person, the manifestation of the wound will either be obviously outrageous like with a Type One who I call the Black and White thinker, (an example of which follows later) or will be more hidden and confusing, like with the Emotionally Dissociated Hero, the Type Three (see the example in the Fan-Hero Family System book under Secret Drama) or somewhere in between with the other Types. Let's look at the most common pattern for Empaths that arises out of the mother wound, and for others as well, based on Positive Shadow and Projection.

The Empath that Puts Others on a Pedestal

One reason the Empath tends to project a very large Positive Shadow is because she sees her faults very clearly, but not her gifts. And so her own gifts tend to be projected outward onto a person to admire. That person soon is seen as if he were without fault or as if he had all-important knowledge. As such, the Empath puts herself in a lesser position, setting herself up as a potential Victim, which makes the other person into a potential Rescuer.

The Empath tends to be dissatisfied with the parenting of one or both parents. Although she may have come to terms with her parents, subconsciously she tends to look for perfect parenting from other authority figures that enter her life, such as new in-laws, teachers, or gurus. Although all of us tend to put people on a pedestal to some degree, the Empath is notable for effusive praise, a need for emotional bonding and a desire to be seen as special when she is fond of someone she admires. Because all people have limits and flaws, at some point the Empath is disillusioned when the parent stand-in does not live up to expectations. This can lead to a cynical and bitter Empath if this pattern continues to serial objects of admiration. However, with each cycle, the Empath has an opportunity to observe the pattern and heal the original wound.

The degree of the wounding from the original parent also makes a difference. If the wounding was severe, subconsciously the Empath longs for a perfect parent, but also knows that that parent is going to let her down. When the parent substitute does prove to not live up to expectations, (no human being can because none of us is perfect), the Empath feels betrayed as she did by her parents. The pain is the same old pain, and can be quite intense. In retaliation, she can reject the parent figure quite violently.

Two of my early clients put me on very tall pedestals. The first client, Kay, loved everything I did, took all my workshops, some of them twice, and was very talented herself in the intuitive arts. When I pointed this out to her, she was half hoping that I was right in my assessment, and half afraid. Then she admitted to thinking that if she could have any practice that she wanted, she would do what I was doing.

This clear insight on her part led her into a practice that was similar to mine but had her special touches and uniqueness. Because she was willing to see that her admiration of me was an indication of noticing unused power and talent from within herself that needed claiming, I did not fall off the pedestal with this client. Instead, the pedestal was dismantled and we became true colleagues and friends with our practices complimenting each other. As she stepped into her niche, she was able to see me more clearly as a whole person. Her feelings of intense admiration diminished into healthy respect and friendship.

Before this Kay had had a string of failed relationships with women that were embarrassing and confusing for her to remember. When we looked at her relationship with her mother, and her unresolved wounds around that relationship, then these relationships with other women began to make sense. Kay's view of her mother was somewhat negative; Kay resented her mother's selfishness. Kay unconsciously went looking for proper mothering, which included and expectation of special attention from other women, especially older women. At first the relationship seemed to operate well, except that Kay gave these women authority over her while thinking that she was behaving as an equal. Kay had unconsciously set it up so that she would be disappointed by these women, just like she had been disappointed by her mother. How Kay set up these relationships to fail remained in the Shadow for her. Eventually Kay was surprised when she discovered that these women did not think of her as equals. Then Kay would leave the relationship feeling taken advantage of and confused.

When Kay came to me as a client, it was obvious to me how she wanted to put me on a pedestal. After she completed my workshops

Kay wanted to continue as an ongoing individual client, but also wanted to maintain a friendship as well. In an effort to not play out her Mother Wound pattern with her, I told her that she needed to make a choice: she could have me as her shaman, or she could have me as her friend, but not both. Given that we had so much in common and enjoyed each other's company, I was very happy when she chose the friendship over the shaman relationship. I also pointed out how she was trying to put me on a pedestal which automatically made us not equals, and that she needed to be conscious of how she was likely to do this in the future with other women. It remains a practice for Kay to be mindful of this piece of Shadow Work but because I took this behavior out of the Shadow at the beginning of our friendship, it is easier for Kay to stay conscious when relating to me.

With my second client, Lynn, she was effusive with praise practically every session we had. She also took my workshops and wanted to explore her intuitive gifts. When I recommended that she see one of my teachers who was within driving distance of her, she eagerly went, hoping to make the same connection she had with me. She reported back that I had more talent and warmth than my teacher did, and I could feel her disappointment that my teacher wasn't as she had hoped. This was very interesting to me, especially since I felt that Lynn would be comfortable following me around as guru to student and not step into her own power.

One of the reasons Lynn did not like my teacher was because that particular teacher has incredibly good energetic boundaries. This teacher did not allow Lynn to put emotional energy into her. The relationship on an energetic level was very clear; Lynn was not going to be able to play out her wounding with that teacher and so Lynn didn't like her as soon as she realized this subconsciously. This particular teacher had no interest in inviting anyone to continue pedestal behavior with her.

When I pointed out to Lynn that perhaps she was putting me on a pedestal, she told me that I simply didn't see myself and my talents clearly. She could have been right, but her response combined with previous behavior was an indication to me that I was in trouble. I had seen Lynn push other teachers that had failed her off the pedestal. One teacher was traded in for another when that teacher didn't live up to her standards. After seeing this a few times over our year of working together, I figured that at some point I would be next. I could see Lynn's Shadow and how she was creating failed relationships with teachers, but she could not.

One of the clues that Lynn had a deep mother wound was how much she praised her mother and how attached she was to her mother. Unlike Kay, Lynn had a lop-sided positive view of her mother, but wasn't conscious that she did, even though it was obvious to me. This meant that Lynn would have a harder time than Kay bringing her Shadow behavior to consciousness because of the extra step of seeing her mother as a flawed person instead of an ideal. When a client must idealize her parent, it usually means that there is some hidden and painful feeling, wound, or belief that the parent inflicted which the client cannot not face. The fact that Lynn was hiding her mother's wholeness from her consciousness was a sure sign some mother wound lay in the Shadow. Lynn had farther to go in healing her mother wound than Kay did.

Lynn praising and admiring me felt wonderful. I enjoyed it, but I didn't take it too seriously because I knew it wasn't real. At some point Lynn was going to become disillusioned with me when she disagreed with me or when she found a teacher she liked better that was willing to have Lynn permanently in the student role. And sure enough, about a year into our work, I fell off the pedestal dramatically as I was traded in for a better guru. Luckily for me, I didn't take it personally because I knew that the rejection, just like the admiration, had nothing to do with me but everything to do with Lynn's Shadow and original wound.

In Lynn's case she was unable to stop the cycle of admiration and disillusionment, and so she missed the opportunity to see within her the places where she was not claiming her authority. Instead, that authority remains projected outside of her in other teachers. Lynn, in effect, will never grow up until she stops projecting her power away onto mother-substitutes. Lynn's Shadow Work lies in becoming conscious that she has created a pattern of admiration and disillusionment. The next step is becoming conscious that she is trying to resolve an old mother wound through substitute mother figures.

Sometimes the best way to get out of the admiration/disillusionment cycle is to experience both roles. As a former unhealed Empath with definite parental wounds, I had done this often enough with authority figures in my life. When I was ready to reject the authority figure, I had intense feelings of anger and betrayal that this person had faults. However, I liked putting others on a pedestal because that person usually made me into a pet, which gave me a place of belonging and a sense of being superior to others because I was in a special position. Some gurus do take pets deliberately as a way of collecting power for themselves from willing participants. However most teachers teach not to collect power but to impart information, but they are still projected upon.

When I first experienced being knocked off the pedestal without knowing that this was a cycle of behavior and was not about me at all, I experienced great pain. First there was shock that someone who had liked me so much could turn so quickly on me, and then there was confusion as that person blamed me and accused me of letting them down, of pretending to be something that I was not, and of plain lying to them. Being an Empath, I felt that person's intense psychic attack, and it took several days to understand what had happened and to recover. Being introverted, I seriously questioned my behavior and if there was anything I could have done differently. There was great danger for me in succumbing to the Empath's tendency to withdraw by giving up my work altogether. It was only with help from more experienced healers that I understood that that person really wasn't dealing with me but was using me to project their wound upon. After that it was very easy for me to catch myself putting anyone else on a pedestal, and to spot others doing the same to me.

Empaths need to look carefully to see if they are stuck in this cycle. Not only does it ruin relationships with the guru figure, but the continuation of it makes sure that the Empath does not claim her gifts and integrate her power from her positive, but unclaimed Shadow. Playing out the Pedestal behavior means being stuck in a cycle of never stepping into full maturity. If the Empath can catch herself at this behavior and own the projection, she has a very good chance of stopping the behavior and moving into her authority. The key is to remember that if she has an intense feeling about the guru figure, that very intensity is probably an indication of projection at work. After noticing the projection, the next thing to do is to tell herself that what she sees in the guru figure also exists in herself. She is really that wonderful!

If you're an Empath with an unhealed mother wound, and you have someone on a pedestal, try to stay conscious that the person on the pedestal is an imperfect human being. The predictable next step in this archetypal pattern is to become disillusioned with the guru. Once this happens remember that this is old anger, pain, and disappointment and has little to do with the person that just tumbled off the pedestal. The guru figure has strengths and weaknesses just like everyone else. Assume that your rejection of this person is unreasonably extreme, because it most likely is. Then go to your nearest shaman and begin working on the old mother wound.

Staying conscious through the disillusionment process can be an uncomfortable experience because it means taking responsibility for a projection while taking on personal power. It means giving up a Victim Stance. It also means stepping out of a child or student role and making oneself stand on equal footing. Giving up the benefits of the student role can be a challenge because it is safe, and there is someone else to lead the way. However, if the Empath can master this projection, she is looking forward to a life filled with more joy and more excitement, and more access to the very talents she loves in the guru figure expressed through herself.

Remember, Empaths are prone to putting others on Pedestals because we have a hard time giving up our Victim Stance. We want others to tell us how special we are, leaving us at the mercy of other people's approval and validation. Once we step fully into our authority, the combination of personal empowerment and compassionate presence means that others will tend to project their mother wounds onto the Empath. Next we will discuss an Empath being put on a pedestal not by an Empath, but by a Black and White Thinker. As we will see, the pedestal is dangerous for both people involved. It is a predictable archetypal pattern—once we can spot it, we can choose how much we want to engage in such relationships. When the projection happens in a friendship, as we will see next, or a partnership, the relationship will be in serious jeopardy unless the projector becomes conscious enough to stop the infatuation/disillusionment cycle.

5 THE BLACK AND WHITE THINKER

Manifestation—We are Creating All the Time

One of the challenging shamanic concepts for the beginner to accept is that we are creating our lives all the time. Our ability to create depends on what beliefs are in operation. Many of us who have been taught that we should be able to create our desires with ease and grace become disillusioned with the Co-Creating process, not understanding that because our belief systems aren't always our own and aren't always conscious, we create unwelcome problems instead of what we want. Most of us are run by a family belief system, archetypal belief systems, the local culture's belief system, beliefs stemming from past-life stories, and finally our own personal belief system. (We can think of past-life stories as stories that live within us or resonate strongly with us.) A look at our favorite movies and books can also point to such ingrained stories and beliefs. It is no wonder that so many of us have a hard time creating what we want when many of the beliefs that run our lives did not begin with us.

    I help my clients examine beliefs that are so ingrained that they feel like facts of life instead of something that can be changed. Once we are able to renegotiate and change our beliefs, we can finally concentrate on what we want to create, based on what our Souls (or Hearts) want, without all the mess and confusion of repeated unhappy outcomes. To create what we want, our Soul or Heart needs to lead the way. We can think of the Soul as that part of us that is directed from the Mythic level, that part of us that is on the

Journey, which is here to learn certain lessons, experience certain events in life, and work out various karmic contracts. When we have a Heart's Desire that we want to manifest in the world, that directive comes from our Soul's Journey perspective.

For most of us in the western world, our Souls do not lead the way. Our Heads lead the way instead. What I mean by this is that our belief systems, our thoughts, and our old patterns fueled by old emotions and by old wounds can lead the way. When we have a faulty belief system (meaning that it gives us unhappy outcomes or is simply untrue) we experience suffering and our creations do not turn out the way we would like. Also, we cannot see the world clearly because of projections stemming from old wounds. Our Vision is distorted, which leads to distorted creations. That being said, we do not want to throw our Heads out—we need clear Vision in order to choose the Right Actions to bring about our creations. Much of the shamanic energy work I do clears wounds at the Heart so that my client can practice clearing his Vision by becoming conscious of the old thought patterns and beliefs. Once he conscious, then he takes Right Action by choosing new behaviors so that he can manifest a different outcome than before he did shamanic work, (usually Soul Retrieval and Underworld Work).

We want our entire system to be clear of old wounds and faulty beliefs so we can begin creating what we really want with our lives in a coordinated fashion. First, our Heart already knows what it wants. Then, our Vision brings down that envisioned or imagined idea, and finally our taking Right Actions manifests our dream at the physical level. Many of us have lost touch with our Hearts so we may end up easily creating whatever our Heads say we should create, but our creations remain unfulfilling. Empathic Heroes and Heroes can fall into this trap as we will see in The Fan-Hero Family System Book.

Or we may be in touch with our Heart and have clear Vision, but be unwilling or unable to take Right Action and so remain stuck. Many Empaths tend to have great Vision but are afraid of taking Action. In this case the best solution is for the Empath to take baby steps toward her goals despite fear and resistance while working on becoming more grounded and on healing old mother wounds.

It may also happen that we are in touch with the Heart, able to take Action, but our Vision is skewed by projection. We are then in a painful bind in which we repeatedly pursue our Heart's Desire, unable to see that our faulty belief system is the cause of our unhappy creations. We wind up creating out of our Shadow. Let's look at Travis's story, which best fits this description, next.

Get to Know Your Stuff, or It Will Get You

Our example, Travis, was a Black and White Thinker (closest to the Type One on the Enneagram). Black and White Thinkers tend to divide the world into Right and Wrong, and they try to make sure they are always Right, or at least always Justified so they can feel Right about themselves. When they get over their blind spots, they no longer think in terms of Black and White and Right and Wrong, but have an internal code of ethics to which they try to adhere. They acknowledge both themselves and others as flawed, and they no longer project their own faults outward. When they give up the Black and White belief system they tend to project their shadow sides less onto others; they see people as complete human beings in which both the Black and the White exist. They can make great leaders, partly because they understand that human nature is flawed, but also that humanity can be capable of great things with a code of principles intact.

Unlike Empaths who make emotional states most important, Black and White Thinkers tend to organize their world around thoughts and beliefs. The Black and White Thinker has a hard time realizing that their belief system is not all important to most people. Similarly, Empaths have a hard time accepting that their emotional state should not be the most important factor in guiding decision and action. As an example, it is typical for Black and White Thinkers to be highly critical but to dismiss the effect their delivery has on the emotional state of the people around them as irrelevant. Black and White Thinkers can be taken by surprise that others, especially Empaths, want nothing to do with them when all the Black and White Thinker wanted to do was help the other improve. Others tend to feel criticized and belittled for not living up to the Black and White Thinker's code of beliefs.

Travis, a typical Black and White Thinker, had many things going for him—he landed a well-paying job after successfully completing a graduate degree, he was smart, attractive, and enjoyed a variety of interests. Travis had created a successful life for himself in a new town away from his original family. Now he wanted to create his ultimate Heart's Desire—a marriage and a community to go with it. However, Travis had to address his biggest block to manifesting this dream—rage. Travis repeatedly had angry encounters not just at work, but also randomly on the road or even in parking lots. At one point three such events occurred in a two day period. Travis complained that people were crazy and unreasonable. A friend suggested that the common denominator here was Travis. What was going on within him that every day encounters turned into escalating angry situations? Travis, unwilling to see himself as the cause of his problems, left in an angry huff.

After enough of these incidents occurred along with a close relative telling him that he couldn't discuss certain topics with Travis because of his anger, Travis to his credit, came back to do his personal work to bring his anger issue to consciousness. The anger stemmed from his childhood, mostly around his relationship with his mother. Travis needed to address his wounds around how his mother did not take care of him as a child so he could get over his rage and stop projecting it onto the outside world. Until he took care of his inner belief system, he would continue to experience conflict in the external world. In other words, Travis needed to clear his Vision of the projection stemming from his mother wound in order to move forward with the relationships he wanted to create with others. Travis had to bring the mother-wound out of the Shadow so he could take a look at it and heal himself by changing his beliefs that stemmed from that wound.

The important point here is that a blatantly obvious pattern of anger showed up in his life instead of the harmonious relationships he wanted. When such patterns occur, it means that WE are creating it. We may not be consciously creating it, but some deep-seated wound and its accompanying belief system are influencing our behavior so that we manifest what we do not want instead of what we want. If we have tried to create our heart's desire, but we fail repeatedly for even apparently unlinked or random reasons, it's safe to assume that an underlying hidden root cause is in action. Each of us is responsible for noticing the pattern as our own instead of blaming other people who are simply playing out their role in the pattern for us. This is the heart of getting out of Victim, stepping off the Drama Triangle and actually cleaning up our lives: it is the heart of Shadow Work and it is also the heart of manifestation. In every moment we are creating our lives, whether we consciously know it or not.

Once again, Travis's mother is not to blame for Travis's rage. (Please see my book on the Archetypal Drama Triangle for a more complete explanation.) It is Travis's responsibility to heal the wound and clean up the accompanying belief system that generates the rage so that he does not carry the rage from that original relationship into his relationships in the present. This is Travis's Shadow Work—he must deal with his rage no matter what his mother does. If Travis concentrates on the wrongs his mother did to him as a young child, he remains in a Victim state, helpless with no chance of stepping into his own authority because he's given it all to his mother in the past. To heal and to step into our authority, we must get off the Drama Triangle, and drop blame, which means dropping the Victim Role. To Travis's credit, he realized that his anger was his own, and that he had to get help to deal with it.

All Women are Placed in the Mother Position

It is important to note that because Travis's wound was so severe, every woman Travis met was put into the Good Mother position, tested to see if she fit, and then discarded if she did not. If the woman didn't fit she wasn't necessarily rejected—she could still be a friend, but unconsciously Travis was looking for something special in women friends; Travis wanted a Mother Figure in his life in the shape of a Big Sis. Big Sis was a woman to whom he could come with his problems, who would be supportive of him, and of whom he could think of as extended family. Big Sis substituted as his mother, with whom he had a volatile relationship.

The danger for his women friends is that they did not understand Travis's hidden expectations. Big Sis was expected to throw his birthday party, to invite him over for Thanksgiving, and to approve of the women he dated. In essence, Big Sis was expected to do everything Travis' mother had never done for him which Travis had wished he had experienced. As long as whomever was playing Big Sis lived up to his expectations, all was well. But because she was put on a Pedestal, the woman friend was doomed to be pushed off at some point—usually when she failed to live up to Travis's expectations of Big Sis.

Enter our Empath. My client had done considerable healing work on her own mother wound and no longer put others on pedestals. She was out of the Victim Position and off the Drama Triangle. As such she had that combination of personal authority and compassionate presence that fit Travis' ideal of Good Mother. Our Empath and her husband liked having gatherings of their friends, liked to plan outings for the children in their group, and enjoyed being the social glue. Our Empath tended to be someone her friends could come to in crisis because, like most healthy Empaths, she was understanding and trustworthy. Our Empath, without knowing it, had become Big Sis in Travis' Vision. Without realizing it she had entered an unspoken contract in which she would take care of Travis' needs until she disappointed Travis. At that point she would be pushed off the pedestal and attacked.

This is important for the Empath to realize—while we are working out our own wounds, we tend to project those onto others in a needy way. When others fail us we can and do attack them, but we also usually withdraw and attack ourselves as undeserving and irredeemable. However, other Enneagram Types retaliate against Good Mother gone Bad Mother with direct and open attack, as we will see with Travis. For Empaths, these kinds of attacks are devastating. It is in our best interests to understand the Mother Wound so we can spot it in action and walk away from the invitation to engage.

Travis and Romantic Relationships

Travis wanted a solid, primary relationship. Given that Travis's rage in general stemmed from his relationship with his mother, it was not surprising that his romantic relationships tended to play out the same mother wound, but in a more intense manner than either his work relationships or friendships. Travis had been through a series of girlfriends with whom at first he was hopelessly infatuated then terribly disillusioned. The breakup usually included angry outbursts from both sides, similar to the disagreements with his mother. Travis wanted a lifetime partner, but he kept reenacting the wound with his mother instead. Every year Travis had a new girlfriend who tended to be subservient and accommodating on the outside. In the beginning of the relationship, all was well. Travis fell in love hard, and the couple spent most of their time together. As the relationship progressed, Travis would find flaws in the relationship and the disillusionment would set in. Finally, as the pattern played itself out, the couple would descend into arguing and in his early relationships, verbal abuse. In Travis's mind the woman was to blame for the failure.

After three girlfriends in a row since beginning his conscious healing work, Travis seemed to be homing in on a better and better match for himself—there was less Drama and more maturity in each successive relationship. Travis was committed to changing his pattern. Travis had learned that even a good match meant a pleasant patch of infatuation followed by a patch of disillusionment and a healthy reality check as real intimacy finally kicked in; in other words he learned about the Pedestal pattern. With his new girlfriend Travis' challenge was to not take the inevitable disillusionment as a sign to break up. Instead it was a sign to truly get to know each other. Predictably, after six months the infatuation wore off and the disillusionment began. Unfortunately Travis could not stay conscious of his pattern to head off the abuse. Travis teased his girlfriend instead of outright verbally abusing her, which was somewhat of an improvement, but his teasing was still emotional cruelty. Travis's girlfriend, although she did not like or deserve the behavior, put up with it. Once again Travis projected the contempt he felt toward his mother for being imperfect onto his girlfriend, but she was not strong enough or willing enough to stand up to the projection. Inevitably the relationship failed.

Travis was embarrassed that now it appeared that he couldn't make a relationship work with a nice person, especially since several of his friends had become attached to this girlfriend and had told him how happy they were for him that he had finally found someone worth keeping. Travis confided to Big Sis that he could use her help—he didn't want to go through this again with yet another woman. Big Sis told him to ignore what other people thought and get on with doing his personal healing work. She asked him what part he played in the failure of this relationship. But Travis did not want to see or admit that he could have contributed to the failure of the relationship. To him, his girlfriend was simply not a good match because in his mind she had been unwilling to be real with him. He thought she was holding back her true thoughts and feelings, so he wasn't having as intimate a relationship as he wanted. In other words, she was deficient. Travis would not look at what it was about himself that made her reluctant to be completely open with him. This is the blind spot of the typical Black and White Thinker—they are Right and the other person is Wrong and the effect of his criticism on her emotional well-being isn't important. When challenged with the notion that they could possibly have done something Wrong, they grasp onto being Right. Notice that his Big Sis did not say that Travis was Wrong, which implies a judgment, she simply asked what Travis's contribution was to the failure of the relationship. Her assumption was that all relationships included two people responsible for maintaining the relationship. Travis's assumption was that someone had to be at fault if a relationship broke up, and that he was not to blame.

Travis, as a Black and White Thinker, tended to criticize, to tease, or to ooze contempt if he didn't like his girlfriend's behavior. She wanted to avoid his contempt, so she held back being her true self. She tried to protect herself from the emotional abuse by appeasing him, but Travis took this as a lack of integrity and openness. He assumed that whatever he didn't like about the relationship stemmed from her flawed character. The problem was that he was attacking her personally, both psychically and verbally, instead of seeing that there was something awry in their dynamic. If only Travis could have focused on the dynamic between them instead of on trying to control her, the relationship might have had a chance to succeed. Otherwise, Travis was fated to create a failed outcome no matter what woman dated him. Together they can work on the dynamic between them, but as long as Travis makes the woman the problem, the only solution is to reject her as unworthy. This is a typical response of a Black and White thinker: if he doesn't like an outcome, he becomes judgmental and the other person becomes bad or less than him. The Black and White Thinker puts others on the highest of pedestals and then knocks them down more than any other Enneagram archetype.

Of course, the reason his girlfriend had held back was because she did not have a place of safety—Travis's contempt toward her eliminated that possibility. Travis had actually put her in a double bind in which he demanded she be genuine, but she could not be her real self without feeling like she was under constant attack and criticism. If she held back, then she was also attacked. If there were any differences between them, then she was belittled and of course there are always differences between healthy individuals. She was doomed: Travis would treat her with contempt no matter what she did. When Big Sis asked if he could allow his girlfriend a soft place to fall, Travis immediately said he could not. Travis's attitude was that she did not deserve such treatment—in other words Travis was withholding a sense of safety for his girlfriend until she lived up to his standards of integrity and openness. As most of us know, no healthy relationship can survive without a sense of safety and trust. Travis's attitude had killed this relationship but he could not face the fact that he had contributed to the failure. From his perspective it literally was all her fault.

Travis had made his girlfriend feel exactly like he had felt when his mother had found fault with him. He had created the reverse role with all his girlfriends in which he was the judgmental criticizer. In the relationship with his mother, he was the one who never felt good enough, who felt unfairly criticized, who never had a place of safety to just be himself, who could never relax in the feeling that he was loved for himself just as he was. He had to strive for perfection; the unfairness and the hypocrisy in observing his mother's flawed behavior set his tendency to rages. Travis in effect was punishing his mother through his girlfriends but was completely blind to his creation. Travis felt perfectly justified in this behavior, even though he repeated it every year, and even though he wondered why his relationships never worked while his friends paired off easily.

The blind spot of the Black and White thinker is to believe that situations and people could be intrinsically bad rather than flawed. Travis was an unhealthy Black and White Thinker in that he and everyone else had to live up to his rigid code of Right and Wrong. Admitting that he had acted wrongly interfered with his feeling good about himself so he had to twist his thinking so he could see himself as Right. As such, Travis could not admit that he was wrong and still see himself as a good person. He was either good or bad. As a result he couldn't afford to fully face his pattern, and so insisted that his girlfriend simply wasn't a good match. Travis was unable to stand the pain of looking at his Shadow and how it caused unhappy outcomes for him.

The Unhealthy Black and White Thinker is Judgmental

Travis asked Big Sis how he could form a lasting relationship with a woman. When Big Sis pointed out the blind spot of the Black and White Thinker, which ironically Travis had studied months before, he became angry. Travis insisted that his girlfriend was friendship material rather than girlfriend material and that Big Sis was defending her. Yet his former girlfriend was uninterested in any relationship with Travis, including friendship, which confused Travis. Travis could not see that women who got to know him found him harsh, critical, and rigid, and as such these women chose to leave rather than tolerate his contempt. Travis unconsciously believed and expected that the women in his life needed to stay and put up with his anger because that was what his mother had failed to do—unconsciously he was trying to complete and resolve his relationship problems with his mother through these women.

The Black and White Thinker has no idea that their ideas of Right and Wrong inevitably make others feel judged and unsafe, including themselves! While any Enneagram Type with as deep a wound as Travis's would have the same mother wound pattern of infatuation followed by disillusionment, what makes Travis's harder for him to see is that as a Black and White Thinker he clings to the idea that there is one perfect way, or one perfect woman out there that will solve all his relationship problems. The Black and White Thinker has trouble doing his personal healing work because looking at the shadow side of himself becomes looking at the Black or irredeemable side of himself. He cannot see the dark side in himself and still view himself as a good or worthy person. Because of his Black and White nature, it is either one or the other. It is much easier to make the other person irredeemable or wrong instead of admitting he could be wrong. Travis has an easier time projecting his mother wound onto other women instead of simply acknowledging the wound and its pattern playing out, and dealing with it. Until he can face the underlying shame that comes with being irredeemable, which is difficult for any human being, Travis cannot heal. If Travis could step outside the mindset of the Black and White thinker and realize that there need not be judgment about his behavior, only objectivity, he might be able to sidestep the shame of being irredeemable.

Unfortunately, our belief systems create our lives, so Travis will continue to repeat this unhappy relationship pattern.

Anyone who feels judged is unlikely to be open and vulnerable with the judger. Travis was in the same bind in which he had put his girlfriend and all his girlfriends—he, too, couldn't afford to be honest and open with himself because he was so judgmental, even with himself. He was stuck in viewing his behavior judgmentally rather than being able to view his behavior objectively. As a Black and White Thinker Travis had to make sure he was never wrong, and so he looked for ways to justify behavior, which often meant a skewing of his perspective so he could make the other person wrong.

Black and White thinkers tend to think everyone sees the world judgmentally in Black and White, so when Big Sis pointed out his blind spot, he assumed she thought he was to blame and that he was a bad person. Notice that Big Sis's intent was to answer Travis's questions helpfully, not to shame Travis or to make him wrong. Travis's belief system does that to him. Big Sis's actions are interpreted through the belief system. No matter how compassionate and loving Big Sis is with her feedback and advice, Travis interprets her behavior as intentionally making him feel ashamed, criticized, betrayed, and like his soft place to fall has disappeared. Travis's mission then becomes to convince Big Sis she is wrong, that she has misunderstood the facts (and him) so he can feel loved once again. Unfortunately what this means is that Travis must shift into trying to control Big Sis. Whoever plays Big Sis in Travis's life is in a bad position, just like all his girlfriends.

Travis could not see that he was creating repeated relationship failures patterned after the relationship with his mother, and that he had to address his contempt issue before any relationship with a woman would have a hope of succeeding. Drama and anger must be the central theme of any romantic relationship until the wound was addressed. Drama is guaranteed for Travis because when someone is Wrong, someone is to Blame, which assumes an abdication of responsibility and personal power. By not taking responsibility for his part in the relationship failures Travis stepped into the Victim Role of the Drama Triangle. He then shifted into the Bully Role by attacking the women in his life that have let him down with contempt and criticism, feeling justified the entire time. Travis is used to the end game of his relationships consisting of angry arguments between

Victims and Bullies. This is the example of connection he was given as a child, and this is what substitutes for a loving relationship for Travis.

Travis's Heart might know he wanted a Real Relationship, and he might be able to take Action—after all he created a new relationship every year—but his Vision was deeply skewed so those relationships turned into a repeat of the pattern stemming from the relationship with his mother. His Vision is skewed by the faulty belief system, the projection—he cannot see women clearly. His Vision of an ideal relationship for himself is a completely unrealistic fantasy because he's looking for a perfect mother in the form of a perfect woman, which obviously does not exist.

The Good Mother Projection can be Hidden

Someone with a deep Mother Wound is always unconsciously looking for a new mother figure. That mother-substitute is then held responsible for making the wounded person feel good about himself. While the mother-substitute fulfills her role well, the person is happy and in love, and all seems well. But all mother-substitutes eventually fail at keeping the wounded person happy all the time, and then the person attacks the mother-substitute for letting him down yet again. This is the typical putting others on a pedestal behavior discussed earlier in this book—Empaths tend to have abandonment issues rather than rage issues with their mother figures. Empaths need to heal their own mother wounds, but it is ironic that Empaths can also experience role reversal like Big Sis with Travis. Empaths fall into the mother-substitute role naturally because we are empathetic and caring, and we are easy to confide in. In Travis's case, because the wound was so severe, every woman he met was first put into the mother-substitute role, including women already with partners. She might have been discarded immediately as unable to fulfill Good Mother, and a relatively normal but not intimate friendship would begin as had happened with some of Travis's friends. But Big Sis had been able to fulfill Good Mother, and so even though she thought she was having a friendship, the closeness that Travis wanted (which Big Sis, as an Empath, gave to everyone naturally by her willingness to be real and open) was based on Travis's underlying need for mothering.

For the whole of Travis's adult life Travis's energy went into finding a girlfriend who would, unknowingly to both Travis and the woman, act as the mother-substitute. The pattern in those relationships took only a year to work itself out, given that couples spend so much time together, and Travis dove into his relationships with his girlfriends very quickly. In a little less than a month Travis was exclusive with his new girlfriend and spent all his free time with her. Eventually the infatuation wore off and the girlfriend went from Good Mother to Bad Mother and the disillusionment and contempt set in.

Travis, with no girlfriend upon which to project, was actively looking for a mother-substitute because during those times when he didn't have one he felt uncomfortable and untethered. This is important: Travis is driven to look for a mother-substitute so he can play out this pattern. His hidden belief system has made his purpose in life that of emotionally abusing women. Consciously what Travis wants is a partner and good friendships. Unconsciously he instead leaves a string of women who hate him in his wake, all while blaming the women for the failed relationship.

The Mother Wound Combined with the Need to be Right

When the next girlfriend entered picture, Travis cautiously observed himself in the relationship. He still could not believe that he was unconsciously looking for someone to fulfill all his emotional needs, and that by doing so, he was unable to see who these women actually were as individuals. He did not want to believe that he never saw them clearly; that they were masked first by the infatuation stage, and then next by the disillusionment stage.

Travis deemed the new girlfriend not spiritual enough, even though she was willing to please Travis whatever way necessary if only he would make that clear. She didn't have needs beyond whatever Travis needed. Ironically the new girlfriend was exactly what Travis's underlying Wound wanted—someone to fulfill his needs—but that was not satisfying enough for Travis because what his Heart wanted was a real relationship. Travis found this relationship boring and dissatisfying with a critical ingredient missing. That critical ingredient was of course this woman's sense of individuality.

A real relationship meant an interaction between two people who had different needs. However, any relationship with a woman who was not focused solely on Travis's emotional state meant eventual conflict, as it does in any relationship because people are individuals. But conflict for Travis was never an opportunity for intimacy because of his unhealthy Black and White Thinking. Whenever differences occurred Travis had to make sure he was Right and the woman Wrong; it never occurred to Travis that both people could be right and not agree. Travis turned conflicts into an escalation of his demands at the expense of the other person's needs and limits.

Travis wanted a real relationship, but his Mother Wound prevented him from seeing the woman in front of him as a real person. His wound drove him to find a woman to fulfill all his needs, but when that sort of woman showed up in his life, the relationship ultimately felt unsatisfying and empty. Travis was trapped in a double bind. He could have an unsatisfying, unfulfilling relationship generated by his Mother Wound, or he could have a relationship that might have worked except the intensity of his disillusionment destroyed any affection both Travis and the current girlfriend had for each other. Travis' Mother Wound influenced negatively all his relationships with women.

The important point is to notice how Travis worked so hard to create his Heart's Desire of a Soul Mate Relationship, and yet the Mother Wound and his Enneagram Blind spot ensure that what he manifests is not what he truly wants because he literally cannot see the problem—his Vision is faulty. When it comes to women, Travis's instincts and intuition cannot be relied upon to give him good direction. Travis will not get what he wants unless he deals with that Mother Wound, and unless he also gets a hold of his need to be Right at the expense of other's feelings. The combination for Travis was particularly lethal in his primary relationships.

The Pattern Plays Itself Out with Big Sis

Big Sis had learned about Travis' mother wound after talking to him about his girlfriends. She understood from our work together that she was in the Good Mother position—there were only two positions to be in as a woman in Travis's life—but she had hoped Travis was conscious enough to keep reminding himself to refrain from giving her too much power over him. However, at a friend's party, Travis called her the matriarch of their group of friends. Later Travis literally began calling her his Big Sis, which to her was just another version of the Good Mother Archetype. When she called him on this, he stated that it wasn't his Mother Projection, she was simply older than he was, and his calling her Big Sis had nothing to do with his mother projection. Big Sis then made sure that it really was Travis's projection—she asked the rest of her friends whether they thought of her as the matriarch of their group of friends. All laughingly assured her that they saw her as an equal and that that was just Travis in typical action. One friend even said that she deliberately smashed any pedestals Travis tried to put her on so she would never fall into Travis's Drama. Another friend thought that Travis had a thing for Big Sis, which could now be explained as maternal rather than romantic.

Travis was disillusioned and frustrated with another new girlfriend six months later. He remarked that their group of friends had several successful couples and he was the only one who had never married. Big Sis pointed out that most of these couples were also best friends. Travis might want to concentrate on making a best friend rather than a girlfriend, which would require him to see the woman as a person. Best friends know, respect, and take into account the other person's needs, they make allowances for foibles and faults, and they do not make demands. If Travis could approach a new woman in this fashion, he might be able to keep his pattern in check and actually break it. Or at least he might be able to keep the infatuation and disillusionment stages from being so intense. Travis agreed that the couples he most admired were indeed best friends.

At another gathering, this time a small private wedding of their mutual friends, Travis spent most of the day throwing irritation and anger towards Big Sis. Although Travis didn't speak it or act on it, our Empath was quite aware of Travis's anger and did her best to ignore it and him. She suspected that Travis was having a hard time with his friend's marriage because this friend was the last single person besides Travis to marry in their group. This friend had done his personal work and almost immediately had found his partner and now was marrying her a year later. Travis had been working hard on his relationship issues for years, and he was still nowhere near a serious relationship, let alone an engagement. The easiest person to throw unconscious anger and frustration at was Big Sis—she had been a target in the past, and she represented the underlying reason (his mother) that Travis had so much trouble in his relationships.

Travis admitted his anger, and he admitted that she had done nothing to deserve it. He knew that it was his Mother Wound up again, and he was frustrated that these old feelings were so intense in the present. At that point Big Sis told Travis he needed to go back to his therapist, and he probably needed to go to a shaman as well, and work on resolving it. He couldn't do it alone, and it wasn't fair to put it all on her. It was affecting their friendship again, and she did not like having to deal with anger that she could do nothing about, especially since she didn't cause it and so had nothing for which to make amends. Travis chose not to do this, probably not realizing how seriously endangered she thought their relationship to be.

Next, Travis asked Big Sis to throw his birthday party. She had done so in the past; in fact, it had become a tradition in that Travis brought his new girlfriend of the year to his birthday parties that she and her husband hosted. The previous year Travis had attacked her for suggesting that introducing his girlfriend at his birthday would not be kind given that she would be the butt of a standing joke among a large group of people she was just meeting. What our Empath didn't understand at the time was that Travis was in effect bringing home his girlfriend to get Big Sis' (Good Mother's) approval. Her discomfort burst a hole in his fantasy about his girlfriend, and about our Empath. In the present Big Sis was not interested in throwing any more parties for Travis. For one thing his party was now associated with bad feelings, and two, it felt too much like the Big Sis role that she had no interest in playing. She gave Travis a firm no even though she felt obligated, and even though she suspected that Travis would hold her refusal against her.

Travis then turned to the other women in their group of friends. Travis wanted a birthday party, and he wanted another woman to throw it for him. Big Sis was not the only woman who felt responsible for Travis's feelings, somehow all the women of the group felt obligated as well. The new woman in the group didn't have a large enough apartment but wanted to contribute food if someone else hosted while another woman who was going through a difficult pregnancy and was not up for social gatherings felt guilty for not wanting to host it. Yet another woman, who was very private so hadn't had any of their friends over to her house, agreed to be the backup plan after Travis told her that it was a great place for a (his) party. Travis had no idea of the trouble and stress he was causing others because no one thought to give him a firm no except Big Sis. If he really wanted a birthday party, why didn't he just throw it himself? The reason, of course, was that Travis's party had become a symbol to him of the women in his group meeting his needs. If one of them didn't throw him a party, then he would not feel loved by his friends. Finally another woman agreed to throw a combined birthday party for her husband and another mutual friend of the group.

After observing the behavior of her friends, our Empath was convinced that Travis' mother wound was deeper than she had realized, given how it pulled behavior out of her group of friends, some of whom were non-Empaths and so not as easily influenced by these hidden patterns as Empaths. I cautioned her to be careful around Travis. Since he didn't have a girlfriend, his projection on Big Sis would be stronger than if he was in a steady relationship.

Next, Travis told Big Sis of his first date with a new woman. He had taken her to a restaurant that another girlfriend had introduced him to, and sure enough that girlfriend (one that he still held animosity toward) was also there. Travis was upset about her presence, but felt he handled his discomfort well by asking to be seated on the other side of the restaurant and then by having a pretty good time anyway. He told Big Sis that he had to accept having such an intense reaction to that girlfriend, and that he didn't expect that he'd ever get over his mixed feelings for her. (Notice the abdication of power here: Travis is a Victim of his feelings) She commented that it was no coincidence that his former girlfriend had shown up—that it was a reminder to do more work on the Mother Wound before it ended up playing out with a new woman. She reminded him to focus on Best Friendship instead of Romance as they had discussed the last time they had spoken.

Travis, expecting Big Sis to be sympathetic towards his bruised feelings and to be proud of him for not letting those feelings ruin his evening, reacted with anger and irritation. Travis told her that he wasn't looking for a Therapist; he was looking for a Big Sis. This is important: Travis's statement indicates that he wants her to meet his needs as he thinks a loving Big Sister would. Big Sis would make him feel good about himself and collude with his Poor Me story. Travis just indicated that he was not interested in doing his work; he expected her to make him feel good about himself and give him a pat on the head. Travis was angry that she was not complying, but instead was making him feel Wrong and not good enough, which of course was Travis's old feelings and had nothing to do with her intentions. Travis had become unconscious of his pattern playing out; Big Sis had done something natural to her that put her into Bad Mother position, and Travis's next predictable action was to force her back into Good Mother according to his expectations.

It's also important to note here that Travis had the hidden expectation that his friend could switch between the roles of Therapist and Big Sis whenever he wanted her to, and she would know which role he wanted her to play. However, this was counter to who she actually was as a person. She could not separate out the roles within her because the whole point of being a healthy human being is to live a real life as herself, free of identifying too strongly with roles and rules—notice this is the complete antithesis of the average Black and White Thinker, who is dependent on a code of rules and is most comfortable when others fit into roles. She was not interested at all in playing Big Sis for Travis. Big Sis was Travis's fantasy that she had fit into well when whatever she said to Travis made him feel good about himself. Travis's complaint indicated that he wanted her to be Good Mother, and he was angry that she was not complying.

She told Travis that he was allowing his pattern to play out again, and he had just attacked her for feedback. She would therefore not discuss his personal life with him, even if he wanted her to in the future. Travis protested that she could not make such a decision without him. He wanted her mirror and he could handle it, he just didn't want it to be so one sided. Basically, Travis wanted the feedback to always be encouraging and make him feel good. Notice what Travis is really saying here: Travis' comment illustrates the blind spot of the unhealthy Black and White Thinker. Travis literally believes that she cannot make a decision about what she says and does without his say so; they must be in agreement in order to be in a relationship that works. Of course the reality is that she can decide and act on anything she chooses. Travis has no control over her thoughts, actions, or feelings even if they are about him. But Travis believes that he does and he believes that she is being unfair and unreasonable.

At this point Big Sis reminded Travis that she only agreed to talk to him about his personal life if he could own the mother-projection, and he was proving that he could not. She also reminded him that if he attacked her the relationship was over, and he was getting very close to the point of outright attacking her. She told him that from her perspective Travis wanted her back in the one-up position of being responsible for his feeling good about himself, and was angry that she wasn't doing so. Travis denied this, saying that he was actually taking her off the Pedestal by not wanting her feedback as a Therapist but wanting her to be Big Sis. He reiterated that he called her Big Sis just because she was older, not because of the mother projection. At this point Big Sis laughed in frustration. Travis was so stuck in his projection that he could not see that his actions were the exact *opposite* of what he thought he was doing. He had also put her in a double bind: she was now only allowed to say things to him that didn't make him feel bad, as if she should be responsible for his feeling good. If she actually acted as herself, then Travis would attack her. Travis then demanded a face-to-face conversation with her. She refused, knowing and telling him that such a conversation was Travis's way of forcing his view and perspective on her, and if she didn't agree, then he would fall into default mode and yell at her. She would not let him act that endgame out with her. She told him that he was about to lose the friendship if he didn't get a hold of himself. What point was there in being friends if she was just there to be a stand-in for his mother, and he couldn't see her for who she truly was as a person? She told him to back off and think about what she said.

This made Travis pause and take a look at his behavior and feelings. Travis said that yes, he could see that he was projecting, and yes, he was trying to keep her on a pedestal, but he did not think it was all projection. He also said he had concerns about her and that he wanted to talk to her husband about them who was a third observer that could confirm whether the projection was in operation or not. At this point she felt so much stress that she realized that the friendship with Travis was nearly over on her side because it was no longer worth the emotional cost to her. She could feel Travis's rage simmering across the cord that bound them together, and she could feel his desperate need to control her and force her to see things his way.

It is important to note the strain this relationship put on Big Sis. Any Empath will feel this type of stress when dealing with someone like Travis. She knew exactly what Travis was up to, and her being fully conscious of it protected her from playing out his Drama with him. She refused the confrontation that Travis needed in order for him to insist on being right and to feel in control. She knew that such a confrontation would eventually lead to the endgame of Travis's relationships: angry confrontation and explosion, with Travis convincing himself that she was the unreasonable bad guy. Even though she was well protected on the physical plane, her fight/flight response was stuck in the on position because she was under direct psychic and emotional attack. She felt very stressed, her heart rate was up, and her body was ready to act as if Travis was about to physically attack her. Travis had mounted a psychic attack even if he was prevented from acting out his Drama on the literal plane. On the energetic plane it was set up to unfold, and her system knew it. She would make sure that it would not happen physically, but there is still danger here and a cost for any Empath in such a situation. Once again, a psychic attack can manifest in the physical body as stress; the stronger the psychic attack, the more the physical reaction in the body.

When Travis met with her husband, he told Travis to stop talking about his personal life with his wife. It made both Travis and her unhappy, so the practical solution was to stop talking and move on. Just as they knew not to bring up politics with certain friends because it made everyone unhappy and put unnecessary strain on the friendships involved, Travis should not bring up his personal life with her and expect her to say anything about it. If he did, then she should come down on him hard, and if she gave him unsolicited feedback, then he should come down on her hard. In one action, he took care of any objections Travis still had about Big Sis being a Therapist and in the one-up position with Travis, to which Travis had objected. But Big Sis' husband also takes care of the real problem, which is Travis putting her in the Good Mother position that Travis still wants unconsciously. Travis had to agree because his friend was so reasonable and the action taken would fix the situation to which Travis had objected: Big Sis being his Therapist rather than just the equal friend he said he wanted.

The hidden communication was that Big Sis' husband refused to engage Travis in further Drama by talking about Travis's view of his wife, and he made it clear to Travis that the relationship that Travis really wanted was not possible. He had also given Travis a new set of rules to operate from that were free from any possibility of engaging her in the mother-projection, which was unsatisfying to Travis, but was the only way the relationship could be salvaged and be healthy. He then encouraged Travis to email or call her, to apologize for putting her under so much strain, and to confirm that he would no longer talk about his personal life with her and expect her to respond in any way. Travis agreed.

But Travis did not contact Big Sis. Travis was dealing with the Mother Wound's old emotions of anger and of needing desperately to put her back into the Good Mother position. His next predictable step in his pattern was needing to put her in the Bad Mother position if he could not reinstate her as Good Mother. But now Big Sis's husband had taken away Mother; Mother had abandoned him. That Mother relationship was completely off the table, and Travis could do nothing about it. It was a point of mastery for Travis to take her out of any Mother position, instead of project that she had abandoned him. Travis was feeling misunderstood and rejected, and thought if only he could only talk to Big Sis face-to-face that he could get her to agree with and approve of him again.

Every night that week, our Empath felt Travis's continual psychic attack. She woke up between 2am and 5am and had to argue with Travis (energetically) to leave her alone. She also had dreams of Travis following her, trying to corner her into a conversation, in which she always managed to escape. Then, one night she had a dream of Travis threatening to torture and kill her. However, he was interrupted and she escaped. She tracked him back to his apartment, and then tortured him the way he had threatened her. She woke up feeling refreshed and happy after having beaten him to death inside her dream. Coming out of the mental fog that usually accompanies psychic attacks and lack of sleep, she finally realized that Travis had been psychically attacking her, and that she had been allowing it until last night when she finally stepped back into power. She did her sandpaintings to hide herself energetically from him. That night she slept without being disturbed.

Unsurprisingly the next morning Travis emailed her, stating that he regretted that it had taken him so long to contact her, and he again asked for a face-to-face meeting so they could talk about their relationship. He had only bothered to contact her on the Literal level because he could no longer keep up his demands and attacks on the Energetic level. Although Travis believed that he was going to establish a healthy new relationship based on equality, she understood that Travis's asking for a face-to-face meeting was just the same abusive conversations he had with all his girlfriends during the end of the relationship, and was all about Travis trying to exert control. More than a week of psychic attack, combined with not doing what he was told would save the relationship, and followed by no apologies or consideration of her feelings after she had specifically told him that a face-to-face was too hard on her, was more than enough to convince her that Travis would only play out his Drama the way he always had done in the past. He wasn't going to get a hold of his projection, at least not with her. Our Empath was finished, not because she didn't love and like Travis, but because Travis could not have a real relationship that was of any benefit to her.

Hidden Communication Rather than Stated Communication

Our Empath made it clear that she would not meet with Travis in person because it was much too hard on her, but she hoped that they would both be comfortable seeing each other at gatherings. What she was really communicating that the old relationship was done, a more distant one must follow, and that she thought Travis wouldn't like it. Travis responded that he would not attend future gatherings with their friends because he would feel too weird with the situation unresolved for him. He needed to speak to her in person. What Travis was really communicating was that he didn't like it, and he wanted to meet face-to-face to see if he could change her mind. Plus, it would be her fault if he didn't come to parties. She responded that she still was not interested in a conversation; if he needed a reminder of her reasons why, all he had to do was look back at their email exchanges. In this way she was really communicating that she wouldn't talk to him any further, and give that Travis had not listened to her reasons that led to that decision anyway, more talk about how she wouldn't talk to him was pointless. Travis responded by saying that he had given up on wanting feedback from her since she couldn't handle it, and he just wanted to move forward as equals. All he wanted to do in a face-to-face meeting was go over the new rules of relationship and make sure that they both felt better. Of course that could have been done in an email prefaced by an apology, which would have made her feel better so there was a hidden reason Travis insisted on this face-to-face meeting. Notice how Travis had started to see her as someone deficient. In other words, he had as his pattern dictated put her into Bad Mother position.

Travis went on to say that he considered her family his family, and that she and her husband and children were what made the city home to him. He thought of and loved her as his big sister. Travis assumed that because he thought and felt about her in this special way, that she would be touched and would change her behavior. He completely ignored her previous objections to being thought of as his big sister; instead of making her feel special, this made her feel uncomfortable. Also, Travis expressed gratitude for the help she had given him over the past five years, and that he wouldn't have made such progress without her Empathic nature. He had to make sure she knew how thankful he was for that, even though that progress was not worth it if it had lost him his family relationship with her. Travis fixated on her being an Empath as the problem, instead of the underlying issue, which was that the qualities that led to her being an excellent confidante also made her easy to put in the Mother position.

She responded that no further discussion was necessary for her to feel better about the situation, and that she wished him well. What she was really communicating was that she would deal with her feelings herself, and she expected him to handle his on his own, as well. At which point Travis told her that maybe a face-to-face meeting wasn't necessary for her, but it was necessary for him; it was who he was and how he processed. Travis was really communicating that he needed to control her, because that was the only way he could feel good about himself, and about any future relationship. He had to have a say in any decision she made about him. But, he was no longer going to insist, she could contact him if she wanted to, since his old way of enforcing what he wanted didn't work. This is an ironic statement since everything he said was all about forcing himself on her.

Most Empaths after reading Travis's response have mixed emotions of anger, of revulsion, and of feeling sorry for Travis. Our Empath certainly had those feelings, but didn't exactly understand why. The reason she wanted to slug Travis was that Travis was still trying to force his view on her even though she had stated that meeting him face-to-face was too hard on her. Travis literally did not care what effect he was having on her; his need to talk about not talking to her trumps her need for space. Travis could not allow her to make a decision to no longer give him feedback because Travis must feel like he is in control. A face-to-face meeting would give him that feeling of control because he would have the opportunity to declare himself Right. In other words, Travis needs the confrontation to feel good about himself. If he didn't get to talk to her one last time, he wouldn't get to state that no feedback from her was the new rule only because he agreed to it. If Travis had truly accepted that she had the right to not give him any more feedback, there would be no need for a face-to-face conversation. If Travis had truly felt that his behavior had been out of line and actually harmful to the relationship, he would have honored both her and her husband's requests that he apologize and give her space. Travis could not see anything amiss in his behavior, so he kept pushing. But she didn't push back like he had expected, and so he was surprised that the relationship failed.

The reason she felt revulsion was that Travis claimed to be an equal and claimed to understand his projection, yet he still called her Big Sis, even though she had told him several times that his Big Sis label bothered her, and that she was not interested in that role. Travis also used his unhappy feelings and discomfort against her; she was responsible for making Travis not feel weird. She was obligated to help Travis feel better by meeting with him face-to-face. No matter what help and insight she gave Travis over the years, none of it had managed to sink in, and yet he thanked her for it. Travis was so stuck in his Mother Wound that he could not see that everything he had said was more proof of how unhealed and blind he was. Travis was willing to use not only emotional blackmail to get what he thought she owed him, but he was also willing to make himself into a good guy when he's behaved like a jerk. He saw himself as the good guy, so she should too.

The reason she felt sorry for Travis was that he was so stuck. He was in the endgame of the relationship, but he's not allowed to play it out like he was used to doing with the blow-up of a few face-to-face meetings in which he would throw contempt and anger at her. So, instead of voicing his rage, which from the Bully position would make him feel strong, Travis was left flailing with no pattern to fall back on. He had only the paltry attack of declaring who he was and that she was preventing him from being himself. He literally could not see that his statements showed he needed our Empath's approval and compliance to feel good about himself. She did not play her part the way he expected. He expected a few face-to-face meetings, a few explosions, and a few reconciliations and then repeat. She had sidestepped the normal endgame of the Drama, and that left Travis feeling very unhappy, confused, and frustrated. Travis was used to having a relationship end where both parties felt so Victimized that they felt justified in Bullying each other with verbal abuse. She was wary of stepping into the Victim role and perpetuating Drama and so refused the invitation.

This was Travis's Drama, not hers. She was free to choose to not engage him. While our Empath was infuriated and appalled (but not surprised) by Travis's response, she resisted the urge to engage him. She also made sure to eliminate all future contact with Travis so she would not be anxious about contact through emails or social networks. Travis could now either go do his work, or go find another mother-substitute. It would no longer be her.

Travis's Skewed Perspective

When we are in the midst of a projection, our perspective is clouded. Others around us may see our behavior clearly, but we literally can't understand the reasons people are responding to us so strangely. Travis felt like our Empath was treating him unfairly, and he felt Wronged by her decision to not give him any more feedback. From his perspective, all he had wanted was for her to treat him as a friend, and that meant she should stop giving him feedback and start giving him Big Sister sympathy.

After she refused to cooperate and Travis was told that they should stop talking about his personal life, all Travis had wanted was to have a face-to-face conversation that would put everyone on the same page and take care of any weirdness. Big Sis didn't get his meaning and assumed that he still wanted feedback when he didn't. They had obviously had some sort of misunderstanding, probably because email was such a poor medium in which to communicate. Now Big Sis was unwilling to talk to him.

How could Big Sis turn on him so suddenly and have nothing to do with him? Obviously Big Sis didn't want to give up the Mother role with him, when all he wanted was to move past that and be treated as an equal. He was a good guy—he loved and valued Big Sis, they had been friends for years, what had he done that it would turn out this way? If he could just meet and talk with her, he could explain himself and his intentions, and all could go back to normal.

Travis was so stuck, and so in need of justifying his behavior as completely rational, well behaved and most importantly, Right, he literally believed the above was what had happened with Big Sis. Despite our Empath explaining to him about the mother projection, and despite Travis actually understanding it intellectually at various points in time, when the projection got out of hand, he literally could not see it or take responsibility for projecting. Because he couldn't see it, he believed that Big Sis shouldn't insist that that was her perspective. The responsibility always lay outside himself and on the woman who was not behaving the way he wanted her to behave.

It is important to note that Travis's fixation on using our Empath as his Big Sis amounted to using her as his therapist. Our Empath, like many Empaths, had been the friend in their group that everyone came to when in crisis. Acting as a support person for most of her group of friends had not done any damage to those friendships because those friends were not deeply wounded. Those friends were responsible for their emotions and their lives and did not rely on her to fix it for them. Our Empath had an area of expertise in handling crisis and in understanding the hidden that was available to her friends if needed. But Travis's wound was so deep that its projection would be intense with most women he met. Any teacher/student relationship, any close friendship, and any love relationship would suffer the same fate as with our Empath. If she had been aware of how deep Travis's wound was when Travis had first begun confiding in her, she would have shut the conversations about his personal life down. But, unfortunately the projection was in play and hidden from her until too late. Plus, much of our

Empath's own healing work was around her own faulty beliefs and blind spots that set up her pattern for friendships with deeply wounded people like Travis, a common pattern for many Empaths, so it is not a big surprise that she needed practice at her own pattern playing itself out and choosing something new. Her typical Empath pattern was walking into these relationships without considering the endgame, even though the endgame was entirely predictable. (See the Fan-Hero Family System book for a description of another Empath falling for the cues to engage in a family drama.) Our Empath was successful in avoiding the endgame this time. Travis will remain stuck until he is able to own his projection and make different choices than what his pattern dictates. Any relationship Travis has with a woman has a predictable outcome.

How Travis Can Heal

Travis's pattern playing out repeatedly, year after year, means that every year he has an opportunity to step back and observe that he is trapped within a pattern in which he is the common denominator. Travis's instinct is to find another mother-substitute right away to ameliorate the feelings of loneliness, of not belonging anywhere, and of being unloved. If Travis can face these feelings, let himself feel them fully, and resist finding a mother substitute, he has a chance of healing the wound, examining the belief system, gaining new consciousness about his behavior, and being able to choose something new in the next relationship. Because Travis's wound is so deep, Travis would benefit from Soul Retrieval and Underworld Work on those Mythic and Energetic levels that traditional talk therapy does not address. Travis can get better, but only if he gives up his search for a woman to make everything better for him, which amounts to finding a woman to fix and control. In other words, Travis must be alone to address himself. As most of us can imagine the process of healing would be excruciatingly painful for Travis, and it would not be a big surprise if he were unable to do so. A few years after our Empath left this relationship, she heard from another mutual friend that Travis had put her in the Big Sis position, and she was no longer speaking to him. Six months after that, another mutual friend also went through the same Big Sis scenario. Both women were very angry at Travis, but after our Empath explained

Travis's pattern, they understood what had played out and could move on without thinking that they were as bad a friend as Travis had made them out to be. When Travis predictably tried to return to these friendships after breaking up with girlfriends (and needing a mother-substitute), all three women turned him down.

If you recognize yourself in Travis, know that you are grievously wounded and that you are the only one that can heal the wound. While others can help you heal, you are the one that will have to face the old painful emotions. Therapy, shamanic work, hypnotherapy, breath work, and other types of healing work are available to help you resolve the old wound. Healing means facing those emotions, finally processing them, and letting the old wound cease to define you. Next, you will have to do the hard work of facing the harm that you have caused others around you by acting out your version of the Mother Wound. Part of Travis's pattern was to punish, criticize, and withhold affection from the woman once she had fallen off the pedestal. His old anger fueled his justifications for such abusive behavior—he literally could not see it as abusive. Admitting we have caused damage (and in Travis's case admitting that he is wrong) is actually a clear action that requires strength and courage. It takes inner strength to be able to contain those feelings of shame, remorse, and regret at hurting those we loved. We must also forgive ourselves and treat ourselves with compassion after we have faced our ugly creation. Finally, accepting responsibility means owning the projection and staying conscious when the urge to play out the pattern arises again. Then we open the door to lasting, healthy relationships between equal adults which ultimately is what each of us wants. With our Vision cleared of this old wound, we are free to create what we truly wanted in the first place.

How to Navigate the Big Sis/Mother Position

What does a woman do if she finds herself in a relationship with someone like Travis? The first point to recognize is that someone like Travis does not care what effect he has on others. He is trying to get his needs met by others, but these needs can never be fully satisfied. What this means is that eventually the people that Travis loves will be seen in Travis's eyes to fail and to disappoint him. It does not matter how much these people strive to care for him in the first place, they can never do enough for Travis. If you find yourself in our Empath's position, a good question to ask is whether you unconsciously believe you should be punished for not living up to unreasonable expectations of perfection. Our Empath didn't believe so, and so took the healthy route and left. But, many Empaths can feel unconsciously unworthy or they feel obligated to stand by the relationship. These Empaths become locked in a Drama with someone like Travis who would gladly reinforce beliefs of unworthiness by exerting control and power. If you recognize that belief system in yourself, shamanic work like Soul Retrieval would be of great benefit in healing the underlying wound and dismantling the faulty belief system.

Travis looks functional. He behaves like a well-adjusted, moral man in most instances until the projection is triggered. When the woman falls into the Bad Mother role, she is doomed to be attacked and mistreated. Travis feels completely justified in this abusive behavior. If you find yourself projected upon as Bad Mother, it is important to realize that that person cannot see you clearly and you must protect yourself as best you can. It does no good to talk to the projector past a certain point, as we saw in this example. Travis was only interested in keeping up a battle, or keeping his Drama going. Exit the relationship as gracefully and as quietly as you can. You cannot fix this relationship. A person like Travis isn't capable of having a real relationship—Travis is intent on a fantasy woman rather than seeing the individual before him.

If you find yourself in the Good Mother role, which can be harder to spot since nothing appears amiss in that there is no obviously abusive behavior occurring, still, it is best to distance yourself from the wounded person. Once in Good Mother, you will fall off the pedestal into Bad Mother, and the abuse will begin. While all human beings tend to put others on pedestals to some extent, listen carefully if there have been a string of relationship failures in this other person's life. If there have been, you are likely to be next, not because of anything to do with you personally, but because of the nature of the Mother Wound. It doesn't have anything to do with you; it is the projector's problem to fix, which means you can never make it better for them, even if they insist you can. This is especially important for Empaths to realize since one of our faulty beliefs is that we can fix anything if we put enough attention on it, even those problems that are not ours.

Our Empath managed to side step most of the end game of Travis' pattern. However, the other friends who were projected upon as Big Sis went through multiple battles with Travis before they rejected him completely. If you find yourself in the Bad Mother position, try not to engage even though someone like Travis will be provacative. Instead, refuse the confrontation and walk away like Our Empath was able to do in the end, saving herself from being devastated by Travis' projection.

6 CONCLUSION

Empaths tend to act out their Mother Wound by putting others on pedestals. We can heal those wounds that propel us to treat others idealistically. Once we've fully stepped into power and maturity, we become easy targets for others putting us on pedestals. My hope is that with this description of the archetypal pattern the Empath will be able to spot this behavior in her current relationship (or old relationship failures), take responsibility by getting help, make amends if appropriate, forgive herself, and move on to Drama-free, happy relationships.

As we can see from the examples in this book, Shadow Work is difficult, confusing work. To do our Shadow Work we need the internal strength to feel bad about ourselves. We need to objectively look at our lives and see if we have created repeated unhappy outcomes, especially outcomes that are the opposite of our intentions. Then we need to stay conscious as we work through another iteration of the pattern so we can change the outcome. Shamanic Energy Work can make this process easier, but mainly it is our conscious choice in every moment to own those projections that makes the difference in dismantling the Shadow.

As we get to know our Shadow and the patterns it creates in our lives, we become more at choice at changing outcomes for ourselves. We are better able to create the lives that we truly want. We are better able to see our effect on the people around us, and we are better able to see the other person's perspective. Doing our Shadow Work makes us better functioning human beings. Doing our Shadow work leads us into being conscious co-creators instead of unconscious co-creators. Imagine what our world would be like if every human being was committed to doing his Shadow Work. I encourage every Empath who reads this book to delve into her work.

My next book, The Empath and The Fan-Hero Family System, addresses the Shadow of a Family System and its individual members and how the Empath can navigate away from such a system. In future volumes I will look more at the Empath's personal Shadow, especially the Father Wound, which has a deep effect on the Empath's romantic relationships and partnerships.

ABOUT THE AUTHOR

Elaine La Joie is a shaman and certified life coach. She has been in private practice since 2002 helping Empaths heal old traumas and patterns so that they can create the lives and relationships that they really want.

Before Elaine opened her practice she worked at the University of Texas Austin in the psychology department and at the Oregon Medical Laser center as a researcher. Elaine holds degrees in physics and applied physics. She realized a few years into this career path that she was jealous of the others researchers who loved their careers. This, plus a psychic opening led her in a completely new and unexpected direction.

Not wanting to advertise as a psychic, Elaine went into Life Coaching instead. She trained with Coach For Life, became certified, and then was horrified when all her clients started asking for readings and training. After a few more years of resistance Elaine trained with the Four Winds Society and later with Marv Harwood of Alberta Canada.

Elaine maintains a limited private practice so she can concentrate on writing. She lives in Oregon with her family. Visit Elaine's website at www.elainelajoie.com for more client stories and resources for Empaths.

Made in the USA
Monee, IL
27 November 2019